C000140510

DISMISS THE CROWD

CHURCH
alive

Dismiss the Crowds

KEN GOTT

WITH
PHILIP LE DUNE

KINGSWAY PUBLICATIONS
EASTBOURNE

Copyright © Ken Gott 2001

The right of Ken Gott to be identified
as the author of this work has been asserted by him in
accordance with the Copyright, Designs
and Patents Act 1988.

First published 2001

All rights reserved.
No part of this publication may be reproduced or
transmitted in any form or by any means, electronic
or mechanical, including photocopy, recording or any
information storage and retrieval system, without
permission in writing from the publisher.

Unless otherwise indicated, biblical quotations are
from the New International Version © 1973, 1978, 1984
by the International Bible Society.

NKJV = New King James Version copyright © 1979, 1980,
1982 by Thomas Nelson Inc.
KJV = King James Version, Crown copyright.
NASB = New American Standard Bible, copyright © The
Lockman Foundation 1960, 1962, 1963, 1968, 1971,
1972, 1973, 1975, 1977.

ISBN 0 85476 882 3

Published by
KINGSWAY PUBLICATIONS
Lottbridge Drove, Eastbourne, BN23 6NT, England.
Email: books@kingsway.co.uk

Book design and production for the publishers by
Bookprint Creative Services, P.O. Box 827, BN21 3YJ, England.
Printed in Great Britain.

Contents

Demolition

1

On the Front Line

It was loud. In fact, it was very loud. The building we were being taken to was being visibly shaken by the battle that was evidently at its most fierce just inside those high walls. Thousands of soldiers were being urgently mobilised and brought in from all over the city to act as reinforcements, and they were now purposefully moving forward to take their place at the front line of the battle that was only a hundred metres from where I was standing. They obviously knew what to expect. This kind of unrest was apparently a regular occurrence in their city, and once again they were returning to take up their position in the ranks. But there was certainly nothing routine or ordinary in what they were engaged in, as far as I was concerned.

This was quite a new experience for me. I had visited many countries around the world during the course of my ministry as a revivalist preacher, and had found myself in many unexpected situations where I was very clearly 'not in control', but I had never before been so close to all-out war on this scale. The strange thing about it was this: despite the fact that I didn't understand the language that any of the soldiers were using, and that I was thousands of miles away from my home and my church, I felt safer here than I had ever felt in any of the countries that I had previously visited. I followed the crowd into the building, quite uncertain as to what I would find when I got inside, but convinced that this was going to be a life-changing experience for me.

The Coliseum, the name of the building into which we were being led, was home that night to a meeting being held by the Youth Cell Network of Misión Carismática Internacional (MCI), one of the four Cell Networks in the world's fastest growing church, pastored by Cesar and Claudia Castellanos. That evening some 20,000 members of their Youth Network were meeting to worship Jesus, proclaim his victory in their lives and wage war on the devil. Nearly 15,000, who weren't so fortunate, having arrived too late to be allowed into the crowded building, had to wait until the following week. The volume of the music was loud enough to make the ground shake, the stage lights were dazzling and the smoke machines were working overtime. The dancers, who led all 20,000 people in a well-choreographed routine of aggressive and physical praise, directed the army of young people in pulling down the spiritual strongholds over Bogota, the capital city of Colombia.

Despite not being able to fully understand what was being said, as the militant praise gave way to an atmosphere of worship that was gentle and intimate I was able to see an abandonment to the heart of the Father and an intense love for the Lord Jesus in the expressions of the thousands of worshippers that were present. That evening the preaching was simple but not simplistic, communicating the word of God to every person present regardless of age or intellectual ability, and the prayers were authoritative, powerful and to the point. The devil was addressed directly with a confidence that he both *heard* what God's people were saying to him and was *bound* to obey. I found myself thinking, 'If I were a demon I wouldn't want to be within a hundred miles of this place.'

I, and the group of leaders that I had brought over from Sunderland, England, soon found ourselves in tears. It wasn't the volume, the spectacle, the number of people who were there or the jet lag that made us weep. It was the fact that God had clearly found a place where he was pleased to have his presence dwell – a place where he felt sufficiently comfortable to stay, and not visit for a short while and then leave. There was something tangibly different in this church from any other I had ever visited, and that evening I knew without doubt that what we were seeing and experiencing was something that God wanted for his church throughout the world. The only question that God was waiting to hear answered was whether or not we would be willing to pay the price that would make this possibility a reality in our own nation.

As I left the building late that night to return to my hotel room, and walked through the crowds of street vendors who sold fried sweetcorn and ripe nectarines to the people attending the MCI events held at the Coliseum, I knew that the decision to follow and obey Cesar and Claudia Castellanos was an essential part of God's future plan for our lives, and we were totally committed to the process of change that this would involve. God had ruined us for ever, and nothing else would ever satisfy the desire of our heart for God to find a house he could call his home, and where we could experience the glory of his presence once again.

The 'set up'

It all began nearly two years earlier when my wife Lois and I were invited to speak at the annual Assembly of God conference held at Prestatyn in Wales. We had heard that Pastor Cesar Castellanos from Bogota, Colombia, was going to be preaching at the conference along with us, and we had been told by members of the Assembly of God executive council who had visited his church in Bogota the previous year that he was the pastor of the fastest growing church in the world. But despite knowing all of this we had no sense of urgency to meet up with him or establish a relationship with him. In many ways he seemed like many other international conference speakers whom we would briefly come in contact with and then never see again. So when we were asked if we would like to meet with Pastor Castellanos for coffee after one of the conference sessions, we agreed to do so more out of a sense of politeness than enthusiasm. But we were completely unaware at that time that this was a Holy Spirit 'set up' and that following that meeting our lives would be completely changed, and changed very much for the better!

We turned up for the appointment a few minutes early and sat in the Promenade bar of the Sands Hotel waiting for him to arrive. We thought that the members of the executive council had probably arranged the meeting so that Pastor Castellanos could hear about what had happened in the north-east of England and in particular the events that had taken place in our church in what had come to be known as 'The Renewal'. After a few minutes had passed Pastor Castellanos arrived with his wife Claudia and their interpreter and they sat down at the table with us as we ordered coffee. After exchanging initial pleasantries we began to talk to them about the things that had taken place in Sunderland only a few years earlier when the Holy Spirit had turned up powerfully and people from all over the world had started to visit us to experience what was taking place and to meet with God. We told him how the meetings had continued every night for nearly two years and how people had met Jesus and fallen deeper in love with the Father, going back to their countries and their churches with a renewed passion for Jesus and compassion for the lost. He listened courteously to everything we had to say, and then looking at us purposefully he asked us what we felt our main 'accomplishments' were as far as the extension of God's kingdom was concerned, and what we were presently doing to build the church in our region.

We thought we were achieving quite a lot by travelling around the world and holding revival meetings in increasingly larger venues, but it quite obviously didn't impress him at all. It was at this point that he spoke very directly to us, in a way that would have been easy for us to take offence had it not been for the transparency of his spirit and the grace with which his message was delivered. He simply said to us, 'Why have you forsaken your entrustments to pursue those other enticements? Can you find it in your heart to dismiss the crowds, go back home and start building the church again?'

Dismiss the crowds

This was not at all what we had expected to hear. The impact of those words was far greater than he could have imagined as I had only recently been preaching a sermon about the entrustments of God and the enticements that distract us from our calling. I knew only too well what the Holy Spirit was saying to us as his words cut into our hearts, but before we had had an opportunity to think of anything to say in response he went on to explain what he believed God really wanted us to do. He told us that within Jesus there was the capacity to dismiss the crowd, and of course our growing ministry at that time was very much a ministry to the multitudes and large crowds. Jesus would often send the crowd away and turn to those the Father had given him out of the world (John 17:6) – his twelve disciples – putting his time and energy into teaching them and pouring his life into them in preference to holding 'big meetings'. Pastor Castellanos told us that God would have twelve people for us, into whom we would be able to pour our lives following the pattern and example of Jesus, and that in time they too would each find twelve people of their own and would do the same. He went on to say that if we were willing to do this, in time we would be able to impact our region for God.

In hindsight I suppose many other people could have given us this advice, but this man spoke like a father to us and we knew that he was not criticising what we were doing, but only wanting the best for us in God. Not only this, but he carried such a spirit of brokenness and humility that we were totally disarmed by it.

Toward the end of our meeting that afternoon I asked if he would pray for us and he agreed. When you have been in the ministry for a number of years you get used to a certain style of praying, the use of certain words and a tone of voice that conveys 'confidence' and 'faith' to the hearer. I expected something of this sort, or at least something with which I was reasonably familiar, particularly from a leader of his stature. And so I prepared myself to receive words of faith and inspiration, of prophecy and exhortation from this anointed and experienced leader of the world's fastest growing church. But I was not prepared for what happened next. When he prayed he simply put his head on my shoulder and began to weep, his tears soaking my jacket as he prayed in Spanish for us both.

The most significant element of this ministry to the two of us was the fact that he was praying from a position of brokenness before God, and it was this that impacted us the most. Something happened at that moment in our hearts that was far more profound and life-changing than anything any well-reasoned intellectual argument could have provoked. Something of the spirit of this man and the Spirit of God entered us and began a new work in our lives, which continues to this day. As he finished praying he said once again, 'Can you find it in your heart to dismiss the crowds, go back home and start to build the church?'

And so began a journey that started in Sunderland and soon made its way into a stadium in Bogota, where we were eager to have more of 'the Vision' revealed to our hearts and were open to whatever the Holy Spirit wanted to say to us.

LIFE APPLICATION

Can you think of a time when the Holy Spirit spoke very clearly to you and in a way that seemed to cut across everything you were doing for God at that time? How did this make you feel? What was your initial reaction?

PRAYER

Father, I am opening my heart to you, surrendering my will to yours. Holy Spirit, speak to me and help me to hear you clearly. I want to know what is in your heart for me. Give me the courage to be obedient, whatever the cost. I ask this in the name of Jesus, your obedient Son.

2

Dismiss the Crowds

Unless the LORD builds the house, its builders labour in vain.
Psalm 127:1

'Dismiss the crowds, go back home and start to build the church'! What are you supposed to say when someone speaks to you as directly as that? How should you respond? And anyway, did he really understand the implications of what he was saying?

I suppose most of us when presented with the need to respond to that kind of challenge might start by counting the cost – or at the very least reflecting on it! By many other people's standards I was a 'successful' conference speaker with a growing international reputation. Only the previous year I had preached at a well-known Bible conference at which 21,000 people had been in attendance. I had ministry trips to Australia, North America and New Zealand booked for 18 months in advance that had all been carefully planned and organised, and for some of these trips plane tickets had already been bought. Was God really asking me to cancel all of these engagements? Didn't he know how much time this would take? And what would the conference organisers think? Wouldn't they take offence at us? Had we been wrong to say 'Yes' to their invitations in the first place?

But that was just the beginning of the divine domino effect that began to spread out in front of my eyes. The ministry that my wife, Lois, and I were responsible for leading, and for which we were known in an increasing number of countries, had a staff of 15 people who depended on our continued conference and ministry activity for their livelihoods. Surely it was impossible to expect anyone as busy as we had become to simply cancel everything, sack our employees, and go back to our home church? Come to think of it, hadn't we just given the church facility away to the local pastor in order to obey God in going to the world? Were we supposed to go back to him and say, 'Well here we are again, back from our travels. Remember that church we gave you a year or so ago? Well, we want it back!'? And what about our staff; how could we let them down like this? Some of them had given up successful secular careers in order to help us in our ministry. Did God really want us to go and tell them we had changed our minds and they would have to start looking elsewhere for employment?

'Dismiss the crowds, go back home and start to build the church'! These are not the kind of words you want to hear when everything seems to be going so well and you appear to be riding the crest of a wave of 'success' in the ministry. But as they began to sink into our hearts, an uneasy feeling developed that perhaps God was not quite as impressed with our 'success' as we were. When Pastor Castellanos spoke to us that day over coffee, the Holy Spirit's life and authority were in his words and we knew that they demanded a response. He was, without knowing any of our personal background or current circumstances, using words that God had already been speaking into our own hearts over the months preceding that conference. When we first began to hear them we had no idea that our whole way of life was going to have to change so dramatically, but there was no denying that this was the Holy Spirit's confirmation that we *had* been hearing him speak, and now God was waiting to see if we would take the next step with him.

Taking the next step

In all the uncertainty of how this was to unfold there was one thing we were sure about: this wasn't going to be an easy process. A lot of things were going to have to die. At the very least we would have to take our 'Isaacs' on a journey up the mountain of sacrifice, without any real certainty that God would not ask us to kill them and actually mean it! We knew without any doubt that there was going to be a high price to pay emotionally. Turning our backs on the conferences that had been such a blessing to us in so many ways was going to be hard enough. Saying goodbye to the godly men and women we had worked alongside during these years, and with whom we had shared such precious moments in God's presence was going to be even harder. Then there were the practical considerations: where would we find enough money to pay our staff, or to feed and clothe our daughters and ourselves? Would we have a church to go home to, or would we have to start right back at the beginning, with a handful of people in a hired hall, with all the insecurity and uncertainty that new beginnings bring?

Obedience

It is at times like these, when you are confronted with a difficult decision to make, overflowing with apparently negative implications, that God brings you face to face with your real motives for ministry and looks to see if you are ready to

move on with him. The bottom line was this: would we obey
God regardless of the implications and the inevitable cost,
or end up accepting second best by settling for the comfortable, familiar and secure? Obedience is a foundational principle when it comes to building the church. The Holy Spirit
had very clearly told us to dismiss the crowd in order to build
the church. Here was the first of many tests of obedience:
either we would build his church in his way or we wouldn't.
There could be no half measures.

The psalmist wrote: 'Unless the LORD builds the house, its
builders labour in vain' (Psalm 127:1). When God says something as simple and obvious as this it is really quite surprising how hard we find it to obey his words and put them into
practice in our own lives. But unless we build his church his
way, whatever it is we're building he won't own. And what he
doesn't own he won't inhabit. God doesn't rent his home, he
buys it outright. If it isn't his church, he isn't coming to stay,
and if he isn't coming to stay – we're wasting our time!

The house of your dreams

Think of it like this: imagine you have just received a cheque
for £10,000,000 as your share in the estate of a long-lost
distant relative who has just died. Suddenly, instead of your
bank account being in overdraft each month by a few
hundred pounds, you are getting personal phone calls from
your bank manager inviting you round for coffee! Your old
school, where you had spent all those years being the last to
be picked for the football team and singled out as 'the person
least likely to succeed' now wants you to speak at the annual
prize-giving ceremony (and by the way they're hoping to
rebuild the swimming-pool this year and would value your
input).

But you have different plans for your new-found financial freedom. All your life you have longed to have the home of your dreams. You have whiled away many hours imagining how many rooms it would have, their relative dimensions, the colour of the carpets and the wallpaper, the number of guest bedrooms, the view from the living room window, the fittings in the kitchen (or the garage!). You have walked around your house on many occasions in your mind's eye. Absolutely nothing has been overlooked in your search for that ideal house to finally settle down in and to call home. And now, after all these years of longing and hoping, your dreams are actually going to become a reality. You have already bought the plot of land that overlooks the densely wooded valley with its meandering stream that you enjoyed exploring when you were younger. So you hire the best architect you can find and he draws up the plans for your house in line with your rigorous specifications, and when everything in the plan is perfect you put the contract out to tender and you employ your master builder. The day comes when you give him the plans, drawn up with great skill and precision by the architect and you say to him, 'I'm going away for a few months to travel the world. I want this place built and ready to walk into when I return.' He promises you he will have things complete by your deadline, and you leave confident that the home of your dreams will be ready to move into in just a few months from now.

Time passes, your holiday is now just a happy memory, and you make your way toward the small village that is near to the plot of land on which your house will now be standing. But something looks odd. You see a large plume of smoke rising from the hill where your new home should be. You try and put this out of your mind by imagining the appearance of your house as you drive up to the front door.

You recall the architect's scale model, with the large window in the centre of the façade, its grey slate roof and red brick walls. You imagine the crunch of your car wheels on the red gravel drive and think of the large white front door with its elegant brass fittings waiting to be opened by you as the proud new owner. But as you drive nearer you begin to feel uneasy. Something is definitely not right! Instead of the white front door with brass fittings there is a lime green door with a large purple wooden handle in its place. Instead of grey slates on the roof there are ugly panels of corrugated iron. Instead of a red gravel drive your car is already sliding over freshly laid turf. Something has gone seriously wrong!

There's no smoke without fire

You try to ignore the large chimney that is belching dark clouds of smoke into the atmosphere and the shed that seems to have been built where you expected the conservatory to be. You are now looking for the master builder who you are convinced must have gone quite mad, and when you find him you are going to give him a piece of your mind. None of these things were in the plans. You walk inside. It gets worse. You have just managed to process the fact that the games room appears to have been replaced by a series of dog kennels (and you don't have a dog!) and the kitchen has been reduced to the size of a broom cupboard. You are rapidly approaching the brink of total despair when the builder appears, a broad smile on his face, and he greets you enthusiastically. 'So good to see you again,' he shouts as he walks confidently towards you. 'Welcome to your new home. I suppose you will have noticed one or two minor changes that we had to make to your original plan, but I think you'll agree they really make the place look so much better. I knew you wouldn't like the kitchen the way you had designed it,' he winks knowingly, 'so we made it more functional and so much easier to keep clean! And what about the games room? Don't you just love that dog kennel theme we've developed in there? We realised that there was insufficient room for all of your dogs so we adapted the design to anticipate the need.'

You are lost for words. This is *not* what you had been dreaming about for all those years. This is *not* what you had spent many hours carefully thinking about and deliberating over. This is *not* what you had been careful to specify so precisely in the design so that you could make this house your dream come true. Whatever the justification for the alterations, whatever the rationalisation for the changes, there is only one thing you are absolutely, unshakably certain about and it is this: you are not going to make this building your home until it is built *exactly* to your specification. Even if the whole place has to be torn down and the work has to start all over again, then that must happen first before you are going to make this house your dwelling place. As far as you're concerned all the hard work of the builders has been a complete waste of everyone's time because the house hasn't been built precisely to your original design.

'You are . . . God's building' (1 Corinthians 3:9)

Why do we think that God is any different? We struggle and compete to build the house of God in the way we think he wants it to be built, but very often we supplement his design to meet our own self-centred ambition, our own need for personal recognition and peer approval. As a consequence, we end up taking the glory for the design, construction process and decoration of the house for ourselves. We think we know better than the One who commissioned the building work, so we trim a little off here and decorate a little differently there. At times we simply do what we think is right, without any reference to the layout specified in the word of God. And all the while we demonstrate our failure to appreciate the high price that God has paid for this project; that it is God who has purchased all the materials necessary for his dwelling place with the life of his Son.

> For you know that it was not with perishable things such as silver or gold that you were redeemed from the empty way of life handed down to you from your forefathers, but with the precious blood of Christ, a lamb without blemish or defect. (1 Peter 1:18–19)

> . . . you also, like living stones, are being built into a spiritual house to be a holy priesthood, offering spiritual sacrifices acceptable to God through Jesus Christ. (1 Peter 2:5)

God does not want us to build a shack or a shed at the bottom of his garden to keep his power tools in until he needs them. He wants to build a home where he can enjoy spending time and being himself! Almighty God is not going to make a shack his home – he's looking for the house he's been dreaming of. He might visit a building that bears a vague resemblance to the house he is looking for, and might even choose to stay for a little while. But only a building that is constructed according to his perfect plan, and using materials bought and purified by the blood of his Son, is good enough for him to make it his permanent residence. God wants a house he can call home. Anything else is a waste of time: 'Unless the LORD builds the house, its builders labour in vain' (Psalm 127:1).

Demolish/rebuild

So often we present Almighty God with the house *we* have built, complete with our modifications and the 'improvements' we have made to his original design, and then invite him to come and visit. When nothing seems to happen in our meetings, sometimes for week after week, we wonder why he doesn't answer our invitations – after all, we've done our very best to make him feel welcome. Of course, that is precisely the problem: *we* have done *our* best. The reality is that from his perspective our constructions are often nothing more than flea-ridden doss houses built on the sleazy side of town, and he isn't going to unpack his bags and stay for any length of time until there are some fundamental changes.

When we realise this, we are immediately faced with two challenges. First, are we willing to allow God to demolish anything and everything that we have ever built that is not according to his plan? Second, are we willing to allow him to start the building process again, this time closely following his design no matter how unusual and unfamiliar it may appear to our eyes?

It follows that if we have been building to meet *our* needs and to make *ourselves* feel comfortable, then a lot of that selfish construction work will have to be demolished in order to make it meet *God's* needs and to make *him* feel comfortable. That may even mean razing everything to the ground that has already been built and starting all over again, depending on how far we have strayed from his original plan! That sounds unpleasant – and it is! *Our* dreams, *our* goals, *our* ambitions will all have to die before he can do anything else. Then, after the necessary demolition has taken place, the Holy Spirit must be allowed to recommence the building in his way, with building materials we have not seen used in that way before, in a style that we are completely unfamiliar with. What would be the point of levelling the ground by putting all those things to death if we simply began to rebuild in our own, old style? Something new must take place, and that will, by definition, be in a different style using unfamiliar materials and building techniques that will inevitably add to our discomfort and insecurity.

Time for the change

For two years I had been busy working for God speaking at conferences all over the world, and by his grace he had used those experiences to forge strong friendships with great men and women of God and to teach Lois and myself more about his power and love. But in my heart I knew that God's call on my life was not to be satisfied by this alone, enjoyable as it was. Conferences are great opportunities to hear what God is saying to his church, but they are not the end in themselves. Throughout my life God has used the conference environment to speak to me about his will for my life, and as I sat with Pastor Castellanos, in yet another conference environment, the Holy Spirit spoke to me again: 'Dismiss the crowds; go back home and start to build the church!'

Build the church, not a crowd

As I began to think about that challenge, I realised that the Holy Spirit was making a distinction between a large gathering of people, the 'crowd', and the process of building the church. Too often, particularly in Britain where church congregations have been small in number for many years, we are seduced into equating attendance with acceptance; the number of people in the pews with the favour of God on the church. But the church was not designed by God simply to function as a rallying point for a crowd of people who have a common interest in life, like the soccer matches that take place on any given Saturday throughout our nation.

Our national media may be happy to represent sport as the 'new religion' of the people, and our local soccer stadium may describe itself in its brochures in spiritual terms that would put many of our churches to shame, but 'gathering a crowd', however big, vocal or enthusiastic, has never been a biblical definition or the primary purpose of the church of Jesus Christ. The Bible uses many challenging metaphors when it describes the church that Jesus is returning for: a bride, an army, a body. Nowhere on *this* side of eternity does it mention a crowd (see Revelation 7:9).

How does God see the church?

Rather differently from the way we do as we survey our congregation each Sunday morning from the platform or pulpit! The Father sees the church as a bride – the bride of his precious Son! A bride is deeply in love with one man, who in turn is deeply in love with her. A bride spends time meticulously preparing herself so that every detail of her clothing is perfectly in place. Her dress is beautiful, spotlessly clean with no blemishes or marks to distract her groom's attention away from her beauty. Her hair has been styled skilfully and her make-up applied tastefully so that she looks absolutely stunning as she walks down the aisle to meet her husband-to-be. The preparation that has gone into making herself ready for the groom is a reflection of her love for him and her longing to please him in every way. No one would expect her to turn up at the wedding ceremony wearing an old dress she had just fished out of the washing basket ten minutes before the service, or without running a comb through her hair, or wearing make-up that had been applied excessively and without the use of a mirror.

And yet we might be excused for thinking that this is exactly what we must look like to the Father (spiritually not naturally!) when he looks at our church. We imagine, and with some justification, that we must look rather shabby in appearance because we know only too well the lack of preparation that has gone into our hearts and lives since the last time we met as a church.

But the Father has the advantage of seeing the end from the beginning. Rather like a person making a complex jigsaw puzzle, who constantly needs to refer to the picture on the box lid in order to remind himself that among this pile of broken pieces lies the potential for a beautiful picture, the Father refers to the image of Jesus when he looks at the church. To the Father we are both beautiful now, and have the potential for beauty when assembled correctly. The writer to the Hebrews (10:14) says: 'because by one sacrifice he has made *perfect for ever* those who are *being made holy*' (italics mine).

The Father sees the final picture, the image of his Son on the box lid ('perfect for ever') and then asks the Holy Spirit to get on with reassembling the broken pieces of our lives in order to complete the building process ('those who are *being made* holy'). Some of the pieces of our lives, which are the living stones of the church, have been forced into the wrong place through our denominational tradition and overly rigid interpretation of Scripture. Others have been incorrectly located by simple misunderstanding of the plan of God for his house, or through our impatience to move on to the 'next thing' without having taken the time to learn the lessons of the 'last thing'. Perhaps it is time for some of these pieces to

be removed and relocated so that he can begin to rebuild the
church in his way and get us ready for the wedding celebration he has planned. If we can accept this, then *we* have a
responsibility to do something about it.

> Hallelujah! For our Lord God Almighty reigns. Let us rejoice
> and be glad and give him glory! For the wedding of the Lamb
> has come, *and his bride has made herself ready*. (Revelation
> 19:6–7, my italics)

The army of God

The Father also sees the church as an army. An army is
united by following a powerful leader and in facing a
common enemy. Despite years of being the 'church somno-
lent' rather than the 'church militant', or spiritual couch
potatoes in the salvation war rather than the heavily armed,
highly trained assault troops the Holy Spirit intends us to be,
Jesus sees us as his army and longs to lead us into victory
against the works of the devil. The truth is we prefer
'Playstation Christianity' to practical Christianity, with
imaginary weapons that only damage imaginary targets
rather than the weapons of our faith which demolish the
strongholds of the devil through their divine power
(2 Corinthians 10:3–4)!

   There is a pressing need for us to rediscover our God-given
authority as soldiers of the cross and to start using it to great
effect in the salvation war. Traditional non-combative
Christianity needs to be put to death in front of the firing
squad of the church that believes the word of God means
what it says. We can only '*fight the good fight of the faith*'
(1 Timothy 6:12) if we first familiarise ourselves with the
principles and practice of spiritual warfare. All peace treaties

and 'deals' with the devil must be revoked if we are to wage the salvation war as the victorious army of the living God. Traditional doctrinal views that reinforce and give strength to the firmly entrenched beliefs of spiritual pacifism will need to be demolished and replaced before God is able to rebuild his armed forces and launch the all-out assault on the enemy's territory. The Father still sees the church as his army whether we are ready for battle or not. We are the only ground troops available to him and we have a duty to complete our basic training and get on with the war.

'. . . without holiness no-one will see the Lord' (Hebrews 12:14)

Jesus calls the church his body. A body is an intricate system of interdependent biochemical and physical structures that require a healthy heart to maintain their life and function. In the face of crippling spiritual heart disease brought on by years of inactivity and a toxic diet, Jesus still sees us as the extension of his presence on earth, his body, of which he is the head. For this reason the Holy Spirit is challenging us to healthy living through lifestyle modification. We must change our diet, those things we allow to go unchecked into the body, and our level of spiritual activity, if we are going to be ready to face the enemy on the front line. A healthy body is a holy body and holiness is a non-negotiable prerequisite to victory.

The common denominator of brides, armies and bodies is the absolute requirement for trusting relationships in order that they function efficiently and effectively. The bride must trust her groom completely, and must be trustworthy herself. The army must trust the decision and strategy of its commander, and he in turn must be able to rely fully on his troops to carry out his orders to the letter. The body must be inter-connected intimately cell by cell if it is to remain healthy and function purposefully. If this trust, based on intimacy with our Head isn't present, we won't hear the Architect correct-ing the errors in our building and we won't build the house God wants to have for his home.

If we needed to return home in order to build the church then it was important that God dealt with us first; that he had permission to demolish those things in our hearts that were not in line with his plans for our life, and that he was then free to rebuild again in the style that he chose. In dis-missing the crowd we had to be careful not to revert to type, but allow him the freedom to build his church in his way, however unfamiliar the building style or materials may appear to us.

Crowds are fickle

Crowds inevitably follow anything that is successful and the church was intended to be God's success story for the world – a means of displaying his great wisdom to the whole of creation (Ephesians 3:10). If we were to build his church why would he want us to dismiss the very people who were attracted to him? Of course, that was not what God was wanting, and it soon became clear that 'the crowd' the Holy Spirit was referring to represented people with an attitude of heart (the 'crowd mentality') that made it almost impossible for him to build the church in the way he wanted. This became clearer as I began to consider the heart characteristics of crowds in the New Testament. These crowds are notoriously fickle. They can be waving palm leaves one minute and baying for your blood the next. They are stirred up by agitators in an instant, and can easily be sold obvious deception as self-evident truth through the plausible words of a charismatic speaker. Crowd mentality is not God mentality nor is it kingdom mentality, because crowds are independent, self-willed, chaotic groups completely vulnerable to the latest fad or popular belief (see Ephesians 4:14).

Whenever a crowd *(ochlos)* is referred to in the Gospels or in the early church it is a negative thing:

- crowds contain religious hypocrites (Mark 12:41)
- crowds are fickle (Acts 14:11–19)
- crowds are the hiding place of unbelievers (Luke 8:51)
- crowds are mockers (Matthew 9:23–24)
- crowds are easily incited to violence (Matthew 26:47)
- crowds are to be feared (Matthew 14:5)
- crowds make bad choices (Matthew 27:15)

And yet despite this, the people in the crowd who called out for Jesus' death were the very ones he came to save. Jesus had compassion on the crowds. He saw how they were harassed and helpless, like sheep without a shepherd (Matthew 9:36). He wept over them and longed that they would experience fullness of life. But he did not take the crowd up the mountain when he was transfigured, or let them see the miracle of new life with Jairus' daughter, nor did the crowd accompany him when he was in the Garden of Gethsemane. The crowd was not present at these times of greatest intimacy with the Father.

And it was no different for the early church. The apostles, too, saw their greatest opposition when they preached to the crowds, as well as their greatest evangelistic 'successes'. But the apostles recognised the truth early on in their ministry: a member of the crowd needs to meet Jesus before he or she becomes a member of the church; they must have a radical encounter with the Holy Spirit before they can become the kind of radical disciple Jesus requires. The chaotic, faithless, 'religious' crowd mentality must be replaced by the ordered, faithful, humble kingdom mentality.

Crowds or disciples?

Perhaps for this reason throughout the Gospels we read of Jesus dismissing crowds. Not because he did not value the individuals who made up the crowd (after all, he dealt with their sick, their demonised and their dead and he longed to gather them to himself), but he knew only too well their extreme reluctance to draw near to him. Most of the politicians of that day (and today it is no different) would have been delighted at having the large and enthusiastic following that Jesus had, and would have seen it as the evidence of their personal success and the justification of their views and lifestyle. But Jesus dismissed them. He knew that crowds were not the answer – disciples were. The reason he dismissed the crowds, who could be so demanding of his time and insensitive to the feelings of others, was in order that he might invest his time with those who were willing to pay the price to follow him and with whom he could build the church – his disciples.

Consequences

Success cannot simply be measured by the size of our church, the number of meetings we can persuade people to attend, the church programmes we run or the size of our television audience. Success in God's eyes can be reflected only by our obedience to the command Jesus has given us: first, to *be* a disciple, then to go and *make* disciples.

Then Jesus came to them and said, 'All authority in heaven and on earth has been given to me. Therefore go and make disciples of all nations, baptising them in the name of the Father and of the Son and of the Holy Spirit, and teaching them to obey everything I have commanded you.' (Matthew 28:18–20)

Despite the way it may sometimes appear in our churches, Jesus did not say, 'Go, and gather as big a crowd as you can manage through your charisma, personal appeal or people skills.' He didn't say, 'Go, and build a big church based on current management styles or business principles.' Nor did he say, 'Go, and if you manage to keep 90 per cent of your people happy all the time you will have fulfilled my command to you.' Jesus *did* say to his first disciples, 'Go, and *make disciples*.' Being a disciple or making disciples is not a function of race, intellect, colour, health, gender or age – it is a function of obedience. Jesus was the first equal opportunities employer. He will use anyone that is willing to say 'Yes' wholeheartedly to his will for their lives.

So here was a challenge from the Holy Spirit for Lois and me: 'Dismiss the crowds, go back home and start to build the church!' Either we obeyed this command, despite the apparent risk, and moved on as disciples of the Lord Jesus, or we didn't.

LIFE APPLICATION

Has the Holy Spirit been speaking to you about an area of your personal life or church life that he wants to change? How long have you spent thinking about the personal cost involved in such a change? What attempts have you made to justify your unwillingness to change? What are you going to do about it today?

PRAYER

Holy Spirit, shine the searchlight of your holiness on my poverty of spirit. Highlight my selfish ambition. Expose my insecurities that have driven me to build your house in the way that I have. Begin the process of demolition and rebuilding that you long to perform. In Jesus' name and for his sake I ask it.

3

Levelling the Ground

'Truly, truly, I say to you, unless a grain of wheat falls into the earth and dies, it remains by itself alone; but if it dies, it bears much fruit.'

John 12:24 (NASB)

We came back from that conference with a determination to allow the Holy Spirit to demolish those things in our lives that needed demolishing, and to let him build whatever he wanted to build in their place, in whatever way he wanted them built. And so began a process of transition that we knew had to begin in our hearts first before it could take effect in the church. For Lois and myself this meant we were willing to have our hearts laid bare before God and to make ourselves open to his correction. We asked him to show us where our responsibilities lay in bringing about the change that he wanted, and to give us the strength of purpose not to hold back or compromise in any area that he wanted to deal with through fear or intimidation.

We began by explaining to our staff those things that the Holy Spirit had been challenging us about, and in a relatively short period of time God had provided alternative employment for many of them and clear direction for the others. This still left us with the challenge of the five church plants in the north-east of England that God had entrusted to us and for which we had ongoing responsibility. Having given their leaders the authority to develop their own vision for their congregation when we planted them out from our church, we did not feel that it was right to simply call them all back together again in order to provide ourselves with a secure base. And so we decided that the best way forward was to allow God to begin the process of demolition and rebuilding in our lives first, and then set about building a church again from the foundations up, using the principles that he was going to teach us.

We cancelled as many of our planned engagements as we were able, fulfilling only those which, for integrity's sake, we were obliged to see through. In fact, our last engagement before we came back home was at Brownsville Assembly of God Church in Pensacola, where revival fires had been burning for several years. Prior to meeting Pastor Castellanos, it had been our intention to launch out into a new level of international ministry from this base, but now we understood that this meeting at Brownsville was to be the place where we were to lay everything down and return to the church that God was calling us to build. And so having been obedient to the word of God in 'dismissing the crowds' we now began to ask God how we were to begin 'building the church'.

Building from the inside out

In the world's eyes our homecoming was far from impressive. For many people in the church it was no different! We began meeting in a hired room in a local hotel, with a borrowed PA and 40 or 50 people made up from previous members of staff, a few of the people who had not been able to settle into our local churches and who were still looking for a place of worship, and some visitors who were just curious to know what was happening. Looking back on it now we can smile at the thought of visitors from around the world coming to our 'home church', expecting to see a large building with a large congregation, but instead finding 50 people in a hotel room without any of the trappings of a 'successful' church. Visitors who had previously heard me speaking at conferences all around the world would come up to me at the end of the Sunday morning service and say, 'We're sure you're doing the right thing,' but their faces would be saying something quite different! To be honest, it *was* a challenge, but we understood that it was all part of God's ongoing demolition process – a 'putting to death' of many of the things that we had previously considered so important. And we knew that in it, and through it all, God was changing the old value system by which we measured the success or otherwise of our ministry, and was replacing it with something we had not experienced before. This new beginning was the Holy Spirit's opportunity to change us fundamentally so that God could begin building us again, this time from the inside out.

This was a very painful time for us both as we frequently wept before the Lord, often spending hours on our faces before him crying, 'All of you and none of me,' fearful that we might cling on to anything that he was so definitely stripping away from us. On many occasions during this period of demolition we became almost fearful of dreaming about large numbers of people in the church, concerned that we might fall back into old patterns of thought or behaviour, or reverting to an old form or model of church growth. But lovingly and patiently the Holy Spirit restored our broken hearts, this time giving us a new understanding of what he was looking for in his church and giving us the assurance that he would be with us in this step of faith.

Old value systems need renewing

Throughout my Christian life I have been actively involved in the church and eager to see it grow and become a successful and significant influence in society. Prior to the move of God that had come to our church in 1994, and which had resulted in 18 months of meetings six nights per week, I had been an ambitious pastor in the city of Sunderland, who knew how to measure 'success' in the church. 'Success' was measured by the size of your Sunday morning congregation, the size of your offerings, and the size of your facility. 'Success' was measured by the excellence of your worship team and the quality of your musicians. 'Success' was measured by the video and audiotape sales of your sermons and the conferences you hosted. With hindsight my definition of 'success' had more to do with *my* need for the external 'evidence' of divine approval (the facility, the furniture, the fabric) and on beating the competition, whoever and wherever they may be, than anything God was actually looking at or was interested in.

Sadly, much of the church throughout the world uses the same criteria as an indication of their success. As a direct consequence of adopting these values a fiercely competitive spirit enters the church, often most prominent at senior leadership level, with disastrous results. Frustrated, competitive, dissatisfied pastors and church leaders look at their church and say, 'If only I had that PA, if only I had that worship team or those members of staff or that building, *then* I would have a successful church.' The devil is only too happy to reinforce this belief in order to further demotivate the work of extending the kingdom of God. 'Of course you can't see your city changed and thousands won to Christ,' he reassures. 'You don't have the facilities to do it, or the equipment, or the congregation.' And all the while he subtly hints that perhaps God isn't quite as pleased with you as he is with the pastor down the road, because *he* has a much better church building (or equipment, or congregation). The fact is that these external things are not what God is looking at when he assesses the health, or otherwise, of a church. Nor do they determine whether or not he can use us to win our city for Christ! We might be preoccupied with the outward appearance but God always starts by looking at our hearts: 'The LORD does not look at the things man looks at. Man looks at the outward appearance, but the LORD looks at the heart' (1 Samuel 16:7).

Building God's house, God's way

Throughout the course of the Bible we see the longing of God to be with those who love him. From the first man and woman, Adam and Eve, with whom God walked in the garden in the cool of the day, throughout the chequered history of the children of Israel, right down to the present day in the church, Almighty God has longed to have a dwelling place among men and women who love him with every fibre of their being. But down through the ages the same barrier prevents this from adequately taking place – the barrier that comes from the sin that so easily finds a place of affection in our hearts. Until this sin is confronted directly and dealt with radically, our mixed motives and worldly ambition will contaminate our hearts, and God will be unable to be intimate with us in the way he desires.

'*I* will build *my* church . . .'

As church leaders we readily acknowledge the command of God to build his house, but we conveniently forget that Jesus said, '*I* will build *my* church, and the gates of Hades will not overcome it' (Matthew 16:18, my italics). It is *his* church, not ours. It must be built *his* way, not ours.

We much prefer to consider our church building projects in terms of structure and organisation, rather than considering the health of our hearts and our relationship with God, because structure and organisation don't make a personal appeal to us to change or to confront sin. But unless the Holy Spirit changes our hearts through the confrontation and eradication of sin, we cannot build Jesus' church in Jesus' way.

We are more comfortable focusing on the acquisition of property and equipment as the evidence of a 'faith' that pleases God, than ensuring that the eyes of our heart have 20/20 vision in order that we might see him and know him better (Ephesians 1:18). Fixing our eyes on these lesser things rather than on Jesus keeps us busy enough to avoid having to face up to the worldly values that lie just beneath the surface of our 'success'. But unless they are exposed to the light by the Spirit of Truth, we may be doing the work of God but we will not be working *with* God.

Regardless of our hours of prayer, fasting, self-sacrifice, commitment and dedication we will only be 'labouring in vain'.

God considers our building projects very carefully

Before the move of God that came to our church in 1994 I used to believe that the Holy Spirit was a 'gentleman'. Like so many other preachers I believed that he wouldn't do or say anything that I might find offensive, that might upset me, or that was against my will. In hindsight that belief was not based on any experiential evidence, but on a traditional church teaching that had its origins in the mists of the past rather than the pages of the Bible!

In fact, the biblical evidence is heavily weighted *against* this belief! So when the Holy Spirit came in power and demolished our perfectly good church, destroying our church programmes, making our meetings run hours over schedule and interrupting the routine of our daily lives, we were obliged to accept that he was God and could do whatever he liked, whenever he liked, whether we liked it or not. After all, it was his church! During this time the Holy Spirit had forcefully challenged us that he wanted his church back – and by then we were only too willing to let him have it. Night after night we learned to depend on him for whatever was going to take place, and we knew that if he didn't turn up there was nothing we could fall back on that would have any real value. It didn't matter that we had visitors from all around the world who were coming to the church expecting to meet with God. If he didn't turn up we were in real trouble, and if he did we were probably going to be in real trouble as well! He was free to do whatever he wanted and that was often very different from our expectations, but we came to appreciate that his way was always the best.

This had been an important lesson for Lois and myself to learn because we were now seeing how fundamental this principle was going to be when it came to building the church once again. The Holy Spirit does not come with a list of preferences but a list of demands – and as the third person of the Godhead that is his absolute right! He does not come in the hope of negotiating the optional extras that could be included or excluded from the church design, but rather stipulates his conditions for occupancy. Now as we approached the rebuilding of the church, we wanted to make certain that with each decision we took we were being obedient to God's will for our lives and for the life of his church. More often than not this was costly and meant putting to death things that we had highly valued in the past so that the work on his house could continue unimpeded. With all the external evidence of success stripped away from 'our' church as we met week after week in that small hotel room, the Holy Spirit was able to address the real areas that needed demolition and rebuilding in our hearts – without us becoming distracted by the mechanics of 'church'.

The house God is looking for is not a human *construction*, but a human *heart*

Why is it that we are so easily distracted from the work that God is really calling us to? Why do we try to build our churches with so little regard for the perfect plan of God? Why do we place such value on the external signs of 'success'? Sadly it is because these things represent the medals we have awarded ourselves for our own personal effort and achievement, the evidence of *our* own 'success' in the task of extending the kingdom. And *our* work and *our* dedication to the construction task deserve recognition even if only from among our own peers! From God's perspective, however, these external indicators that we place such emphasis and importance on are not really worthy of comment.

The Holy Spirit makes this clear through the prophet Isaiah:

This is what the LORD says: 'Heaven is my throne, and the earth is my footstool. Where is the house you will build for me? Where will my resting place be? Has not my hand made all these things, and so they came into being?' declares the LORD. 'This is the one

I esteem: he who is humble and contrite in spirit, and trembles
at my word . . . ' (Isaiah 66:1–2)

Isaiah tells us that *God* has already made all these things, and
not us (see verse 2). The psalmist tells us: 'The earth is the
LORD's, and everything in it, the world, and all who live in it'
(Psalm 24:1). Why would God be excited at the prospect of
living in something that is already his by right? Our buildings, our facilities, our equipment all belong to him anyway.
They are not ours, however hard we worked to raise the
money or sacrificed to build them – they are his. But God
does get excited at the prospect of living somewhere that is
not already his possession, somewhere that requires the complete and willing surrender of all claims of ownership – and
that place is our heart! The prospect of possessing our hearts
as a place to make his home brings the Father great pleasure,
and the heart truly submitted to him is the only real basis for
'success' as far as he is concerned.

As Lois and I spent time listening to the Holy Spirit, it
became very clear that there were areas in our hearts that
needed his attention – and that he was not going to be gen-
tlemanly in the way he dealt with them!

Grade A building material is the only material he will accept!

Having asked the rhetorical question 'Where will my dwelling place be?', God goes on to give us his answer: 'This is the
one I esteem: he who is humble and contrite in spirit, and
trembles at my word' (Isaiah 66:2). The Hebrew word for
'esteem' that is used here is the word *nabat,* which means 'to
look intently at, to examine closely, to consider carefully'.
The first time this word is used is in Genesis 15:5 when God
tells Abram to '*Look up* at the heavens and count the stars –

if indeed you can count them.' Then he said to him, 'So shall your offspring be' (Genesis 15:5, my italics).

In other words, God was saying to Abram 'Take a close look at my promise to you, Abram, consider it intently and don't let it slip from your thoughts. Keep the vision I'm giving you at the forefront of your thinking – don't let it out of your sight!' Every night as he looked into the sky, the last thing he saw before falling asleep was a powerful reminder of the promise of God to him about his descendants. He may have tried to count the stars; he may have wondered about their nature or simply praised his God for their beauty, but he could not ignore them.

Now God tells us in this passage in Isaiah 66 that he sees us in the same way. He is looking intently at us, considering carefully whether or not he can find a home in our hearts and in our church where he can come and dwell in all his glory. He esteems the man or woman whose heart will provide the necessary building material for his house. The qualities that God is intently searching for in our hearts are far removed from those things that we appear to value so highly and consider the evidence of our 'success'. The signs of 'success' that God is looking for in our hearts and in the hearts of his church are these: humility, brokenness and the fear of God, because these are the hallmarks of a true disciple. These are the attributes he cannot ignore! 'This is the one I esteem: he who is humble and contrite in spirit, and trembles at my word' (Isaiah 66:2).

Humility

Humility of heart is more appealing to God than the 'quality of our worship team' or the size of our main sanctuary. In fact, taking pride in our accomplishments and achievements is more likely to be an offence to God than a delight to him. Adverts which say, when reading between the lines, 'We have the best worship team in the city (so why would you want to join that other church?)' or 'Our youth work is the most radical you will find (certainly better than that other church nearby)' display a great deal about our own definition of 'success' as well as our attitude of heart toward the body of Christ. We would do well to remember that God opposes the proud but he gives his grace to the humble (James 4:6; 1 Peter 5:5).

Almighty God is at home among the humble. When the Father was looking for a woman who would be able to give a 'home' to his Son, Jesus, he found Mary – unremarkable in the eyes of the world, but delightful in the eyes of God.

> And Mary said: 'My soul magnifies the Lord, And my spirit has rejoiced in God my Savior. For *He has regarded the lowly state* of His maidservant; For behold, henceforth all generations will call me blessed.' (Luke 1:46–48 NKJV, my italics)

The Father had 'regarded the lowly state' of Mary and he knew his Son would feel at home in her womb. He had seen her humility and had found everything that he had been looking for to provide a human 'dwelling place' for his Son. If the Father required such humility from Mary so that his Son could live in her body, why would we think he requires anything less from us if his Son is to live in his body, the church?

Brokenness

Brokenness is not an attractive proposition in the eyes of the world. Shops do not advertise 'First-class broken china on sale here'. Garages do not sell 'best quality broken vehicles'

or 'broken gear boxes'. But God places a high value on brokenness: 'The sacrifices of God are a broken spirit; a broken
and contrite heart, O God, you will not despise' (Psalm
51:17).

When talcum powder was first manufactured, the label on
the front of the container used to read 'This talcum is made
of contrited stone' – stone that had been ground so fine that
its powdered residue could float on the surface of water. God
not only looks intently on the humble heart, he also looks
intently on the contrite heart – the heart ground so fine by
the Holy Spirit that it retains none of its previous characteristics. God considers as 'successful' a church that lives in
Holy Spirit brokenness, a church that retains none of its previous stony, hard-hearted characteristics.

Fear of God

The fear of God is not a negative concept. It does not refer
to a sense of terror experienced in the presence of a wrath-
ful and vengeful deity. Fearing God has to do with reverent
submission, the appreciation of the might and majesty of
the One who created everything and sustains all things by the
word of his power, that produces intense love for him and is
demonstrated by willing obedience in our lives. Fearing God
is an attitude of heart that acknowledges the true nature of
the One we serve and worship, and results in us turning our
back on evil. God esteems (looks intently at) the man or
woman who fears him. The psalmist says: 'But the eyes of
the LORD are on those who fear him, on those whose hope is
in his unfailing love' (Psalm 33:18).

Fear of God and love for God are inextricably linked.
God confides in those who fear him (Psalm 25:14), so if we
want to know how God wants to build his church then we

must start by learning to fear him, because he shares his heart with those who recognise him for who he is.

Revival must begin with the broken church before it can reach a broken world

God can make his home among people who possess the heart characteristics of humility, brokenness and the fear of the Lord. In fact, he can make it nowhere else. These are the Holy Spirit's conditions for an acceptable place of residence.

Isaiah writes this:

> For this is what the high and lofty One says – he who lives for ever, whose name is holy: 'I live in a high and holy place, but also with him who is contrite and lowly in spirit, to revive the spirit of the lowly and to revive the heart of the contrite.' (Isaiah 57:15)

If we are serious about revival we must take this verse seriously. Revival must begin with a broken church before it can reach a broken world. No number of programmes, structures or organisations will of themselves change the hearts of the multitudes that are on their way to hell. None of the external signs of success that we value so highly and that symbolise our 'faith' and 'works' will bear any real fruit unless our proud hearts have first been ground down to fine powder. The Holy Spirit is searching for the humble and the broken-hearted man or woman in whom he can live and with whom he can share his heart. As long as competition remains within the church, and in particular among the leaders of the church, there is no room for revival because there is no room for God. But a heart that has been ground fine by the Holy Spirit, and that embraces humility and the fear of the Lord, has no room for competition or worldly applause. In such a heart the Holy Spirit has already inspected the building, made his report to the Chief Architect and levelled the ground flat so that he can start the reconstruction process. When the playing field is as even as that, when our hearts have been broken up and levelled flat, then competition is seen for what it really is – an offence and an obstacle to the work of God in our life as well as our church.

Search me, O God, and know my heart; Try me, and know my anxieties; And see if there is any wicked way in me, And lead me in the way everlasting. (Psalm 139:23–24 NKJV)

LIFE APPLICATION

What was the last competitive project you were involved in? What situations or relationships inside or outside of the church make you feel as though you must prove your worth by being 'bigger and better' than others? What is your attitude to the 'church down the road'? What are the underlying motives for those feelings?

PRAYER

Father, please change my heart by the power of your Spirit. Where there is pride let me experience the true brokenness, humility and holy fear that you long for. Destroy the spirit of competition that has taken up residence there and replace it with the spirit of grace. Make my heart an acceptable dwelling place for your holy presence; somewhere where you not only want to spend time but where you would choose to stay. Amen.

4

Dying Is a Painful Process

*I die every day – I mean that, brothers – just as surely as I glory
over you in Christ Jesus our Lord.*

1 Corinthians 15:31

For many weeks our fledgling church met in that hotel
room, and for many weeks God met with us and challenged
us to 'die well' as we allowed him to expose those areas of
our hearts that needed putting to death. There were times
when this process was very uncomfortable, and those who
had come to join our 'successful' ministry were soon faced
with their real motivation for being there. Rather like a
patient who sees the surgeon's knife approaching the
abscess, and knows that the pain of the procedure will be
worth it in the end, so we found ourselves challenged by the
approach of the Holy Spirit as he came to deal with the
issues of sin that were just beneath the surface in all of our
lives. We knew that at any time we were free to get off the
operating table and run for safety, but that if we did the sin
would be left to fester until its effects spread throughout the
body. And so we determined that, having come this far on
the journey and having been obedient to the word the Holy
Spirit had spoken to us, we were not going to be distracted
from the vision that God had given us – to be a people with

whom he was not only pleased but in whom he was able to dwell. And if that involved some discomfort or even pain as the Holy Spirit 'lanced the boil' then it would be well worth it in the end.

Dying is contagious!

We soon discovered that we were not the only leaders God was killing! After several months the Holy Spirit challenged us to approach the leaders of three of our church plants to see if they would be willing to die to their pastoral ambition and God-given local vision in order to see something much larger take place in the region. One by one we met with them, sharing with them what God had been speaking into our hearts, and we asked them to go away and pray before making a response. Each one agreed to allow God to put to death their plans for their churches and to make the necessary steps to reunite as one church. Each one of those precious men and women laid their churches back down at our feet with a trust that was truly humbling. But we understood that there must be a death before there can be a resurrection, a Good Friday before an Easter Sunday, a sacrifice of obedience before the fire of God falls, and that we were going to have to go through the process of death before the new life would appear.

Over the course of the next few months each congregation was told the reason for the action that was being taken, and in time the new church, known as Metro Church, came into being. Clearly there were some who wondered what was happening, and others who wondered why it needed to happen at all, but the Holy Spirit was blessing what was taking place so that despite the struggles and the pain of change, almost all the people were willing to follow the call.

Life is dependent on change – and change is painful

The process of drawing in the individual churches took time. There was no way that this major undertaking could be rushed because we were aware that God was moving at a different rate and in a different way in all of our hearts. But we were convinced that the Holy Spirit had told us to do this and the willingness of the leaders of these churches to die to their own vision only served to confirm this, so we were committed to seeing it come about.

The Holy Spirit challenged us about the way in which these churches had been started. We had given the leaders the responsibility and mandate to build their church but had then left them to get on with it while we packed our bags to travel the world, only returning between ministry trips with enough time to do some emergency fire-fighting before leaving for another distant location. We had had little time or opportunity to guide them or correct them in the building process, and as a result there were things in each of the churches that were the product of faulty workmanship which only demolition would correct. In addition to all of this, the sense of abandonment that had been generated by our apparent preference for international travel was far in excess of anything we had appreciated at the time, and while this had never been our intention we knew we needed to repent of this to them individually. Again, this was part of the humbling work of the Holy Spirit in our hearts, but we were more than willing to submit to it because we did not want to make the same mistakes again.

But it would be untrue to say that everything was entirely straightforward as a result of these decisions. Abraham may have agreed to take his son Isaac to the mountains of Moriah in order to obey God by sacrificing him, but with each step he took on that three-day journey he had the opportunity to turn round and head for home. Every step of his journey brought him nearer to the place of absolute obedience and sacrifice where his heart was to be tested to the limit of its endurance. In the same way our willingness to die to our hopes and dreams for our churches, and our often selfish ambition, had to be walked through and some days this was more painful than others. Some days we died more readily than others. But together we knew that God had been waiting for this to happen and that death must take place before the resurrection could come.

How are you feeling?

I was talking with one of my friends one day who told me of his experience working as a junior hospital doctor in one of our local hospitals. As part of his training he had been a member of the 'crash team' covering the coronary care unit of the hospital as well as being ready to respond to emergencies on the hospital wards. The specific task of this team was to resuscitate people who had suffered a heart attack and who were in immediate danger of dying if no one was there to help. Whenever the crash bleep would go off, day or night, he and the team of doctors and nurses on duty would run to the place where the person had collapsed and attempt to revive them. Many were effectively dead when he arrived, their hearts having stopped beating and their breathing having ceased. Quickly and efficiently they would assess the condition of the patient, clear the airway of any obstruction, insert needles into the veins to give the drugs that were indicated, and look at the monitor to see what was happening in the heart. If there were no signs of activity coming from the heart, they would begin cardiac massage. He told me that this was applied much more forcefully than was depicted on the television dramas and the reason was simple: the doctor was trying to squeeze the heart hard enough to pump blood around the whole body and to do that considerable weight had to be applied over the correct part of the rib cage. Sometimes the force of this massage resulted in some of the patient's ribs being broken through the sheer pressure being applied to their breastbone. I wondered at the time why he was telling me this but he finished by asking me this question: 'Ken, what is the difference between a man who has just died and a man who has just been revived by re-starting his heart in this way?' I thought for a while but had to acknowledge that I didn't really know the answer to his question. 'The answer is simple,' he went on. 'The man who has been revived is now in much more pain than the man who is dead.'

In the light of what we were all experiencing in the church, I could readily identify with that illustration. The Holy Spirit was applying pressure in exactly the right place and with exactly the right force to our hearts so that he could revive us once again. I knew that the heart of God was for revival and I had spent the last three years preaching that very thing to the world, but now Lois and I were experiencing the reviving work of God in our own hearts – and it was painful!

The vision of the dam

Not long after our return from Colombia during a time of prayer, the Lord showed me a vision of a dam. Behind the dam was a large reservoir of water and in front of the dam small streams of water trickled through a series of sluice gates located at various levels in the dam wall. The streams that emerged from the sluice gates ran together to form a small river that flowed into the valley beneath and disappeared into the distance. There were families eating their picnics together on the river bank and obviously enjoying themselves, while others were engaged in water sports such as canoeing and sailing. The dam and its sluice gates were clearly controlling the supply of water to the valley, and for those who were enjoying their riverside activities they were a reassuring presence. Then I was taken to the top of the dam where I saw a large wheel that controlled the sluice gates. When the wheel was turned one way the sluice gates would open and the flow of water would increase; when it was turned the other way the sluice gates would close and the water supply would decrease. As I looked more closely I saw that there were a pair of human hands working the wheel that controlled the flow of water down into the valley.

'Multitudes, multitudes in the valley of decision!' (Joel 3:14)

At this point the Holy Spirit showed me the meaning of the vision. The dam represented my heart and the water behind it the infinite resources of God. The hands that gripped the wheel so tightly were my controlling hands – the hands of controlling leadership. I personally governed the amount of blessing that the people in the valley were allowed to experience. Those who were able to get to the river enjoyed it and were having a great time, but what about all the others? I realised that this was the valley of decision and there were multitudes that needed to be exposed to the cleansing power of the river of God. The small trickle that came through those sluice gates was never going to be enough to satisfy that multitude!

Then I looked up and saw that each of the sluice gates had a name written over it. One of them read 'brokenness', another read 'humility', another 'vulnerability' and yet another 'transparency'. There were many more names over many more gates but I had seen enough to know what God was saying to me. The degree to which my heart was broken by the Holy Spirit determined the flow of water coming down from the reservoir and spilling out into the valley. And in the same way, the degree to which I had allowed the Holy Spirit to humble me determined the flow of water from that sluice gate, again adding to the flow down into the valley.

Looking back at the wheel I saw much larger, more powerful hands, the hands of God, prizing my hands off the wheel and loosening my control. As he saw my brokenness of heart, his hands, rather than mine, turned the wheel and more water flowed into the valley through that sluice gate. The effect of opening that sluice gate was to allow more water to flow down into the valley, but it seemed so little in comparison to the needs of so many people. Then God spoke to me: 'Imagine what would happen if this was multiplied many times over and I had access to all of your hearts in this way. Imagine the force of the river if all of the sluice gates in the dam wall were thrown wide open! Imagine how many more people in the valley of decision would be able to get into the river.' I quickly realised that as long as the hands on those sluice gates were the hands of controlling leadership rather than the hands of God, the people in the valley were going to be deprived of the resources that God wanted to make available to them. But as those hands were loosened by the Holy Spirit through our willingness to die to our own ambition, the sluice gates could be opened wide and the thirst of the people in the valley met. It was clear that God had a long way to go before the gates of our hearts were not obstructing his resources, but the prospect of what he wanted to do encouraged us to persevere through the painful process of the Holy Spirit resuscitating our dying hearts.

The competitive pastor's 'favourite son'

Stephen was a man full of faith and full of the Holy Spirit
(Acts 6:5) who was chosen by the apostles to serve food to
the Grecian Jewish widows. He had the qualities that most
pastors nowadays would either find very threatening to their
own position or would use as the evidence of *their* 'successful' leadership. But Stephen would be most unlikely to be
found waiting on tables in any of *our* churches, because we
would consider him far too important for that kind of
responsibility. Other people could be left to do that, but
Stephen would need to be given the opportunity to develop
his ministry gifts under the covering of the local church leadership. In addition, Stephen had many other very useful gifts
with which to bless the church: 'Now Stephen, a man full of
God's grace and power, did great wonders and miraculous
signs among the people' (Acts 6:8).

Stephen was the answer to the competitive pastor's
prayers. Not only did this man *not* want to steal the limelight,
being willing to do the menial tasks around the church, but
he was also capable of performing great wonders and miraculous signs among the people. Think of the kudos that would
come to the church (and for that matter, to the pastor) when
the general public found out that he was one of the members.
Think of the publicity that these miraculous signs would
undoubtedly generate, to say nothing of the TV interest, the
viewing figures, the merchandising potential and the income
generation for the ministry. Stephen was a man to be fostered
and looked after, and he would need a salary and a title to
reflect his importance in the church hierarchy. Perhaps he
should head up the 'department of miracles' or take over the
role of chief intercessor in the church? His prayers and peti-
tions clearly seemed to have a certain resonance with the

Almighty! There was one significant flaw in his character, however: he spoke first and thought about the consequences later. Thankfully, God always seemed to step in and rescue him just in the nick of time by giving him the ability to argue his way out of the tight corner he had just managed to put himself in to (Acts 6:10). But that one weakness was more than made up for by his incredible gifting. And a little controversy does tend to keep you in the public eye – after all, no publicity is bad publicity.

Offended by the truth

But perhaps it was only to be expected that he would inevitably fall from grace. One day he just went a few sentences too far and his opponents decided it was time to silence him. And so they very successfully framed him with a trumped up charge of speaking blasphemy against God (Acts 6:11–13), a charge that had previously proved so successful in dealing with disruptive and rebellious heretics similar to him (Matthew 26:59–65). Unfortunately, instead of just admitting that he was wrong and asking them to forgive him, or even acknowledging that some of the things he had said could have been expressed a bit more diplomatically, he just kept digging a hole for himself – a hole that was soon to become his grave. His defence started out well – it's always useful to get the people distracted from the real issue by thinking about the patriarchs: after all, who can argue with them? But the tactful approach didn't last too long and soon he was in hot water up to his neck as he continued his assault using language that sounded as if he was speaking on God's behalf. The tide really turned against him when he started implying that Solomon's Temple wasn't actually the place where God lived:

'However, the Most High does not live in houses made by men. As the prophet says: "Heaven is my throne, and the earth is my footstool. What kind of house will you build for me? says the Lord. Or where will my resting place be? Has not my hand made all these things?" You stiff-necked people, with uncircumcised hearts and ears! You are just like your fathers: You always resist the Holy Spirit! Was there ever a prophet your fathers did not persecute? They even killed those who predicted the coming of the Righteous One. And now you have betrayed and murdered him – you who have received the law that was put into effect through angels but have not obeyed it.' When they heard this, they were furious and gnashed their teeth at him. (Acts 7:48–54)

That really was the final straw. He had traded his final insult, and it wasn't long before the crowd, who had only recently been amazed at his demonstration of miraculous power, joined forces with his accusers to become judge, jury and executioner. In a moment stones were raining down on the blasphemer as the crowd mercilessly carried out its sentence against him, until in one bloody, bruised heap of broken humanity he breathed his last. In one afternoon Stephen had changed from being the 'star' of the church into the scar on the face of the church, which no amount of cosmetic spin was going to disguise. In short, the competitive pastor's 'favourite son' had just become his worst nightmare!

The person God can use to build the church

Of course, there were no competitive pastors in the early church; nor for that matter were there any 'ministries' to support. So what was really going on here? Why was a man as blessed by God as Stephen treated in this kind of way? And why did God apparently abandon him to the crowd and allow this to happen? To understand this we need to remind ourselves of the kind of heart that God is looking for – the quality of heart in which he is able to come and dwell and make his home. The man or woman whom God esteems is the one with the humble heart, with the broken spirit, and with the heart that fears God more than man. Stephen was such a man.

Humility

Stephen's humility was without question. Despite being used by God to perform notable miracles and great wonders his *ability* did not affect his *humility*. He understood that his public ministry was not a *reward* for his humility; it was a *consequence* of his humility. Humility is one of the sluice gates on the dam that God longs to open. When our hearts are humbled before God and our fellow man, God can open the sluice gate wide and the people we meet reap the benefit of God's blessing that flows through our life. When we take the glory for ourselves the sluice gate closes and the vast ocean of God's blessing is cut off from the poor and needy. Only pride would make us think that a man dying of thirst should pay more attention to the pipe that supplies the water than the water that will save his life. Whenever the channel of God's blessing becomes more important than the source of the blessing itself, God shuts down the flow for he will not share his glory with another (Isaiah 48:11). Stephen's heart was a sluice gate thrown wide open to the infinite resource of God's mercy and grace, and the city was exposed to the power and love of Jesus as a result.

Fear of the Lord

Stephen feared God much more than he feared man. You don't win many friends by calling people who are baying for your blood 'stiff-necked, spiritually uncircumcised murderers of the Messiah who resist the Holy Spirit'. Such straight talking does not go down well with religious hypocrites. The tragedy was that what he was saying was entirely true. God was speaking to their hard hearts and telling them that having the dead flesh of their hearts cut off (symbolising their sin) was the only way they could be acceptable to him. The reference to circumcision would not have gone unnoticed by these men of religion who would have heard the threat that was implicit in the use of those words. The prophet Jeremiah had said to their forefathers:

> Circumcise yourselves to the LORD, circumcise your hearts, you men of Judah and people of Jerusalem, or my wrath will break out and burn like fire because of the evil you have done – burn with no-one to quench it. (Jeremiah 4:4)

Stephen was clearly threatening this angry mob with the judgement and wrath of God if they did not repent of their sin. But far from this being an act of hysterical bravado on the part of Stephen in the face of a hopeless situation, this was an accurate description of his accusers as seen from God's perspective. Stephen was a man who 'trembled at his word', and reckoned the cost of displeasing God greater than the cost of displeasing man. No wonder that the Holy Spirit was free to flow through him in such power.

The fear of God is a sluice gate in the dam of our hearts that, when fully opened by the hands of God, releases the convicting power of the Holy Spirit which either drives those who hear his words further into the arms of God or makes them recoil, sending them deeper into the death grip of the devil.

Brokenness

As Stephen's body was broken by the rocks that were hurled at him, he became a prophetic sign to the crowd of what God requires in the life of a man or woman in order to make their hearts his home. The willingness to be broken for the sake of Christ is the subject of very few sermons in the Western world. Martyrdom and suffering are not glamorous topics and are unlikely to produce a popular tape series. But Paul had this to say to the Philippian church some years later: 'For it has been granted to you on behalf of Christ not only to believe on him but also to suffer for him' (Philippians 1:29).

Suffering for the sake of Christ was seen as a privilege in the early church, not a handicap; a sign of victory, not an indication of defeat caused by a lack of faith. Jesus had said to his disciples:

> If anyone would come after me, he must deny himself and take up his cross and follow me. For whoever wants to save his life will lose it, but whoever loses his life for me will find it. (Matthew 16:24–25)

Stephen understood this and was willing to be broken and to lay down his life for the sake of his Lord, who had shown his love for Stephen by being willing to die for him. The death of Stephen was a prophetic sign, not just of brokenness of body and willingness to die for the sake of the gospel, but of the kind of heart that Jesus is looking to make his home in. Such brokenness makes room for the glory of God to descend, and Stephen saw it:

> But Stephen, full of the Holy Spirit, looked up to heaven and saw the glory of God, and Jesus standing at the right hand of

God. 'Look,' he said, 'I see heaven open and the Son of Man standing at the right hand of God.' (Acts 7:55–56)

Stephen was demonstrating his obedience as a disciple by being willing to take up his cross and follow the example of his Master, just as Jesus had commanded. As Stephen made way for the glory of God to be revealed in his life through his humility, fear of God and brokenness, he was given the privilege of seeing the approval of God in the face of Jesus.

The applause of heaven

Soccer plays a very important part in the life of many people who live in our region, with three significant local teams taking part in the league championships every year. Every Saturday during the football season the faithful followers of each team stand in line to get into the ground where their season tickets have already secured them a seat. Before the game they sit talking with their neighbours about their hopes for the game that day; who they think may score the winning goal and what the final outcome will be. The moment the referee's whistle blows they sit in anticipation on the edges of their seats, anxiously hoping that the players on their team will perform up to their expectations. As their favourite player breaks free of the opposition's defence and gets closer to their goal, the crowd collectively move forward on their seats, anticipating the final shot that will put their side into the lead. The attacking player skilfully out-manoeuvres the defenders and unleashes a blistering shot toward the opponent's goal. The goal keeper is no match for the power of the shot, and the ball cannons into the back of the net as the people rise collectively from their seats cheering, waving, shouting and applauding the victorious player.

In Hebrews 12:2 we read:

Let us fix our eyes on Jesus, the author and perfecter of our faith, who for the joy set before him endured the cross, scorning its shame, and sat down at the right hand of the throne of God.

Jesus is seen here, having won the victory over sin and death, now seated at the right hand of the throne of God in all majesty. But Stephen sees Jesus *standing* at his Father's side. What was it that brought Jesus to his feet? What occurrence on earth brought the business of heaven to a standstill and brought a new song of praise to the lips of the angels? What event had taken place that made the King of kings rise from his throne and look intently at something so wonderful that the whole of heaven was captivated by it? Nothing more than Stephen, a man outnumbered, alone, abandoned to his captors and willing to die for the God he loved to serve. This is the man God esteems (looks intently at). This is the man the court of heaven rises to applaud, that delights the heart of Jesus more than anything else. A man who has a humble heart, a broken and a contrite spirit and who fears God more than he fears the opinion or hatred of man.

Whose applause do we seek?

One of the major challenges of leadership in the church involves communicating the heart of God to the people we are responsible for without compromise. Often, when God places vision in our hearts we realise that in order to birth that vision we are going to upset a number of people in our church. Immediately we are faced with three choices:

- Do we ignore what God has said completely?
- Do we implement it immediately without question and wait for the shrapnel to start flying?
- Do we compromise to a greater or lesser extent on the detail because we fear the response of man?

Very often the third option is the easiest path to negotiate. We allow the fear of man to determine the degree to which we are obedient to the word we have received. 'Mrs Jones might be offended (and she gives the biggest tithe in the whole church),' we reason. 'So perhaps I could modify it slightly to make it easier on her.' 'Mr Smith would be furious if I implemented this change – you know how he likes things the way they are,' we plead with the Almighty. 'Perhaps we should hold back on that idea for a little while (you know what kind of influence he has over the other elders!).' When we act like this we are willing to substitute the applause of heaven for the applause of man; a tragic reflection of our state of heart. We may rationalise it by saying we are thinking about the feelings of the flock, or that God hasn't called us to abuse the sheep, but disobedience is still disobedience. In church leadership, as in many other areas in life, the applause we seek determines the choices we make.

As a leader in the early church, Stephen sought heaven's applause and died in order to hear it. As leaders in the church today, whose applause do we seek and what price are we willing to pay to hear it?

LIFE APPLICATION

Whose applause do you seek? When you last obeyed a specific word God spoke to you, what did you spend the most time thinking about or reflecting on afterwards: the praise of man or the applause of heaven? What areas of compromise have you allowed to take up residence in your heart primarily because of the fear of man? What are you willing to do about it?

Consider the following statement:

When St Ignatius of Antioch was considering the threat of martyrdom and being 'Ground into fine flour by the wild beasts' he said, 'Now I can begin to be a disciple of Jesus Christ.'

Adapted from a quote in *The Cambuslang Revival* by Arthur Fawcett (Banner of Truth Trust, 1996)

PRAYER

Father, help me to prefer the sight of your face to the expression of the crowd. Help me, Holy Spirit, to be honest with myself and with you. Let my love for you be the overriding motive behind my obedience to your word. Amen.

5

Humility and Obedience

Humble yourselves, therefore, under God's mighty hand, that he may lift you up in due time.

1 Peter 5:6

The contractor's sign advertising '120 luxury executive 2- and 3-bedroomed flats in this exclusive development' had been in place for the past few months, and the workforce that had been hired to complete the building work appeared to be busily engaged each day as I drove past in my car. As far as the neighbours were concerned the workers turned up every morning, passing through the old entrance gates of the community hospital that they were demolishing (the only recognisable feature of the previous building they had left behind) and at 5 pm they left through those same gates with another day's work completed.

In the first few days of work the progress had been impressive: walls were knocked down, rubble bulldozed and an endless stream of trucks took the waste out through the gates, only to return some time later ready to collect some more. But nothing much seemed to have been going on for the last few weeks. There was certainly no sign of the 120 'luxury executive flats' that were being proudly advertised on the sign. What exactly was going on behind that fence?

To an experienced builder the answer would be obvious. There is a time in every demolition and rebuilding process when the ground has been levelled flat and all trace of the old building has gone but no new building has yet started to appear, or at least none that is evident to the casual observer. Unknown to all but those involved in the building work, new foundations were being dug in preparation for the new structure. The time being taken on the foundations was time well spent because the strength of the foundation would determine the strength and potential size of the structure that would be built on it.

New foundations for a new building

During those early months of transition in the church we began to understand the challenges of not just building the church, but in first allowing its demolition so that new foundations could be laid. When this two-stage process begins, everything that is safe, comfortable and familiar starts to disappear and for a while there seems to be nothing substantial to replace it. This is a time fraught with potential danger because the casual observer (or church member!) is correct in their observation that more appears to have been lost than has been gained.

But appearances can be deceptive. The foundation that is being laid needs to be meticulously prepared. Its depth and strength will determine the size of the church that can be built on it. There is, however, a particular need for courage among the leaders of the church when this stage of the building has been reached, and this courage can only be maintained by constantly reminding ourselves of the vision that God has entrusted to us. We began to appreciate the need for this as the churches came back together again. Some of our people, not unreasonably, wanted to know why everything they had grown to love about their local church was being destroyed when we still only appeared to have the sketches of the design for the new thing that God was going to build. Those with more analytical minds had the greatest difficulty with this and they wanted to know the far end of everything before they would commit themselves to this new vision. The truth was, for much of the time we only understood in principle what the Holy Spirit wanted to do with us. And since he didn't seem to want to elaborate on the detailed outworking of his plan at that time, we were not in the position of being able to explain to the church 'the next step' with the precision that some demanded. And somehow when we admitted this to those who were looking rather doubtfully at what was happening it didn't seem to reassure them very much! Some admitted later that they thought we were making it all up as we went along! But even in those areas where the rebuilding process was more evident, the materials and style of rebuilding were very unfamiliar to many of us, and it took some time for the body of the church to grow in confidence and start moving forward together again.

Abram leads the way!

When Abram was called by God life started to get really interesting for him and his family!

> The LORD had said to Abram, 'Leave your country, your people and your father's household and go to the land I will show you.
>
> 'I will make you into a great nation and I will bless you; I will make your name great, and you will be a blessing. I will bless those who bless you, and whoever curses you I will curse; and all peoples on earth will be blessed through you.' So Abram left, as the LORD had told him . . . (Genesis 12:1–4)

Imagine the challenge that faced Abram as the leader of his family: 'We have to leave everything that we are comfortable and familiar with immediately. Come on, we're going right away!' I'm certain that must have provoked a few questions! 'Why?' his family might have had reason to ask. 'Because God says so!' he could have truthfully replied. 'How do you know God has said so?' they ask. 'Because he spoke to me about some stuff that's going to happen in the future. Don't worry, it's all good news. Sarai and I are going to become parents (and yes, I *know* we're past it!) and that's going to be the start of us becoming a great nation. Anyone who blesses us is going to be blessed by God and anyone who curses us had better look out! There, what do you think of that?'

I wonder how many of Abram's family thought he had lost the plot altogether? Could he give any kind of explanation as to why God had decided to choose him over many thousands of other people who were available when he was so evidently unsuited to the role of fatherhood at his time of life? And how did he know it was God who had spoken to him and not just the result of overeating and a disturbed night's sleep? Could he please outline the 'next step' on his way to becoming a blessing to all nations on earth? What was God planning to do after he had been 'obedient to the word' and packed his whole family off on what sounded like the most hare-brained journey they had ever heard of? So many questions to answer! Abram must have had to resort to patient explanation on many occasions. No wonder God decided to help him out by giving him visual aids!

He took him outside and said, 'Look up at the heavens and count the stars – if indeed you can count them.' Then he said to him, 'So shall your offspring be.' (Genesis 15:5)

'I will surely bless you and make your descendants as numerous as the stars in the sky and as the sand on the seashore.' (Genesis 22:17)

Abram had to keep the promise of God before him at all times, and even more so when his family began to ask if he was certain that he knew exactly what he was doing, as they must surely have done on more than one occasion. Only by personal reflection on the promise of God to him and patient explanation and re-explanation to those who had not received the vision firsthand was he able to lead his family into their inheritance.

Once again these basic principles of church leadership needed to be employed in our church if God was to take us into *our* inheritance in *our* region. We wanted each of the decisions that we took in the demolition and rebuilding programme of Metro Church to be based on our desire to receive the applause of heaven rather than the applause of man. But we knew that we would need patiently to explain and re-explain the vision that God was unfolding to us if we were not going to jeopardise his plan for us as a church. We recognised that this was a highly critical time in the life of the church and that the next few weeks and months would dictate whether it would continue to live or would die altogether. A lot was going to be determined by our own obedience to the vision God was giving us and our conviction not to be influenced by the doubts and fears of some of those around us.

God wants 100 per cent obedience

One Sunday morning, having outgrown the hotel room that we had started out in, I was preaching in our latest venue, an old church hall located in a nearby seaside town. God spoke to us very clearly at that meeting through something that happened to me during the sermon. The platform in that hall was a small area raised about 30 centimetres above the main floor, and it was cluttered with a combination of musical instruments, loudspeakers and cables. I was preaching on the subject of obedience to the will of God and was concentrating more on what I was saying than where I was going! I started to say, 'Even 98 per cent obedience to God is not enough . . .' and as I got to this point I lost my footing on the platform. I stumbled forward, lost my balance and fell off the platform, landing awkwardly. Fortunately I was not injured, but it *was* a humbling experience! The significance of it was not lost on Lois, however, who immediately informed the entire church that God was saying, 'If we don't give him 100 per cent obedience we will fall!' That event, simple as it was, served to reinforce the challenge that the Holy Spirit was bringing to us as a church, to obey God whatever it was he was saying, and however unfamiliar it may appear to our eye.

Later, as we drove home from the church, the Holy Spirit brought further revelation to our hearts about the significance of what he had shown us. He was saying to us that if we didn't give him 100 per cent of our obedience then we would fall from the platform that he was building for us in our nation. It was not that our fall would be the result of moral failure or gross carnality, but that it would be a fall nevertheless, and one that was undignified, embarrassing and public. We took this warning very seriously. It was important that as God was doing something new among us we did not allow pride to creep into our hearts, and in so doing put our hands back on the controls: 'Pride goes before destruction, a haughty spirit before a fall' (Proverbs 16:18).

The death that killed the church

It is said that 'big doors swing on small hinges', meaning that apparently insignificant events are the means of disproportionately large changes in the nature of things. The martyrdom of Stephen was an event like this. On the day Stephen died the early church was changed irrevocably, and with such explosive violence that, had anyone in the church had the foresight to see what God was about to do, most, if not all, would have suddenly discovered many good reasons for taking their summer holidays earlier than usual that year:

> On that day a great persecution broke out against the church at Jerusalem, and all except the apostles were scattered throughout Judea and Samaria. Godly men buried Stephen and mourned deeply for him. But Saul began to destroy the church. Going from house to house, he dragged off men and women and put them in prison. (Acts 8:1–3)

Stephen, representative of the church leadership of that day, made choices that won the applause of heaven but resulted in the destruction of the church! On that very day a great persecution broke out against the church with all the hatred and violent intensity of the ethnic cleansing that we have seen taking place on our television screens. People were dragged screaming from their houses; children were forcibly separated from their parents; sick and elderly relatives were left to look after themselves. The whole church was persecuted with a systematic cruelty that was masterminded by a religious bigot called Saul, who had given approval to Stephen's death as he stood guarding the executioners' robes (Acts 7:58).

No wonder 'godly men buried Stephen' – it's quite possible that the rest of the church had suddenly forgotten

Stephen's amazing ministry with all its healing and miraculous demonstrations of God's power, and were instead
wishing he had never shown up at all. Only 'godly men' could
see the significance of what he had done and why he had
done it, and they honoured him for it, being willing to identify with him even as they buried his body. The rest of the
church probably had a very different view as they tried to
come to terms with the violence and fear they were now
being exposed to. As far as they could see, the consequences
of this hothead's outspoken behaviour were entirely negative
and unbelievably far-reaching in their effect. In one moment
of holy passion Stephen had:

• destroyed a perfectly good church organisation that had
  been growing rapidly by the day;
• brought a storm of violent persecution upon all the families within the church;
• made the church an object of scorn and ridicule among the
  city dwellers;
• changed the structure of the church from something that
  they were familiar with and with which they were becoming increasingly comfortable into something entirely
  without structure, unrecognisable, unfamiliar and uncomfortable.

How many of those early Christians would have had the prophetic ability to understand this event for what it was? No
one could have anticipated what God was preparing to do
next, and which all hinged on there being a man like Stephen
in the right place at the right time who would do everything
the Holy Spirit wanted him to do regardless of the cost.
Unknown to Stephen he became the demolition ball that
knocked down the walls of the early church that were

already threatening to contain them in Jerusalem. God was able to use his radical obedience to transform the region by bringing people in touch with the gospel of Jesus. Even though he faced misunderstanding and rejection by the church, most of us would probably agree that, in hindsight, it was for the best because 'those who had been scattered preached the word wherever they went' (Acts 8:4).

The brokenness of Stephen had far-reaching effects that spread quickly, producing a widespread brokenness in a church that had only recently begun to find its feet in society. The violent hatred that had been directed at Stephen was now being directed with the same ferocity at the church as Saul systematically destroyed it. But the final out-working of this brokenness could not have been predicted by anyone other than God. Powerful, convicting, effective, city-shaking evangelism was the immediate product of the broken church, and this was typified by the deacon Philip, Stephen's co-worker, holding a revival in the city of Samaria (Acts 8:4–13).

The last place on earth for God to move

Samaria was a region that was despised by the whole of the Jewish community. There were no day excursions from Jerusalem or retirement homes for the aged Pharisee in Samaria. Travellers from Jerusalem preferred to make a detour of many miles around the whole area rather than set foot in that region, such was their loathing of the people who lived there. Perhaps because of that it was just the sort of place Jesus felt drawn to! When he passed through Samaria on his way home to Galilee, he met a woman at a well in the Samaritan town of Sychar. She was amazed that he wanted to talk with her because she knew that Jews did not associate with Samaritans (John 4:9). The reason for their hatred was that Samaria was the seat of rebellious worship in the Jewish mind, and therefore probably the last place on earth that any self-respecting Jew would have chosen to visit through the fear of contamination through association.

But whatever the feelings of the Jewish community towards Samaria, the force of the persecution now levelled against the church drove Philip to this despised city where revival exploded. Because the church was now broken they found that they had a new authority in God in direct proportion to their degree of brokenness. Devastating brokenness allows God to release devastating power through the church: demons were publicly cast out, people were healed, and many were saved, baptised and added to the family of God. Satan was publicly confronted and overpowered, counterfeit miracle workers were exposed and those involved in demonic worship were set free from the power of darkness. The brokenness of the church produced great joy in a city that they would not previously have considered visiting, let alone think of establishing a church in (Acts 8:8).

Change is here to stay

Then, at the very height of the revival, just when we would have been suggesting to Philip that he should be considering moving his ministry into more permanent accommodation, the Holy Spirit took Philip out of the meetings. Why would he do that? Surely he could see the kind of crowds that Philip was drawing and the effect these meetings were having on city life? Why would he take such a prominent leader of the revival into the desert at such a critical moment? Didn't God know that only a few wild animals and the occasional tree lived out there? Of course he did! But God had something much more significant for Philip to get involved with. An important official, the minister responsible for the economy for Queen Candace of Ethiopia, was travelling home and he needed to have some questions answered about his own salvation!

Philip, like Stephen, did not let his *ability* affect his *humility,* nor did he let his *ability* influence his *availability* to God. He understood that his public ministry was not a *reward* for his humility but a *consequence* of his humility. He feared the word of God more than the word of man, so when the Holy Spirit said in effect, 'Dismiss the crowds and leave the meetings to the others I have appointed' – he left! No doubt there would have been some who wondered why he was leaving at such a strategic time for the new church in Samaria. But Philip had the same heart as Stephen, and he sought the applause of heaven over the applause of man. He walked out of those Spirit-charged meetings not because he understood the 'next step', but because he feared God too much to do anything else.

What do we want?

Very often our desire for a 'successful' church is the very thing that stops God from being able to move in power. A successful church in God's eyes is a broken church and a broken church begins with a broken leadership. Healthy growth only comes through brokenness. How many of us when faced with the word of God to leave an explosive church growth situation would have chosen to stay in Samaria rather than obediently go into the desert? How many of us would have demanded that God reveal 'the next step' before we agreed to dismiss the crowds attending a successful revival? And, having made the decision to be obedient and go, how many of us would have then spent hours mulling over the things we had left behind while we looked hopelessly at the desert road in front of us?

We may earnestly desire the spectacular healings and miracles, the confrontation and victory over demonic powers and the liberation and salvation of our city and region, but what are the real motives behind our longing for this to take place? And even if our motives are pure, are we willing to pay the price that makes *this* kind of 'success' possible? We simply cannot have the resurrection power we seek, and which God wants us to have, without first submitting to the crucifixion of our fleshly nature. Paul understood this when he told the Philippian church:

> I want to know Christ and the power of his resurrection and the fellowship of sharing in his sufferings, becoming like him in his death, and so, somehow, to attain to the resurrection from the dead. (Philippians 3:10–11)

Intimately knowing Jesus and the power of his resurrection depends upon an equally intimate knowledge of, and sharing in, his sufferings. Discipleship of the kind that Jesus requires is dependent upon us carrying our cross daily (Luke 14:27) and to the people in Jesus' day that meant suffering, shame, pain and ultimately death.

Normal service will *not* be resumed

Philip never did go back to those revival meetings. After he had been obedient to the Holy Spirit and the Ethiopian official had been saved he was moved on to a new location: 'Philip, however, appeared at Azotus and travelled about, preaching the gospel in all the towns until he reached Caesarea' (Acts 8:40).

Suddenly it must have become clear to the leaders of the early church exactly what Jesus had meant when he appeared to them after his resurrection:

> So when they met together, they asked him, 'Lord, are you at this time going to restore the kingdom to Israel?' He said to them: 'It is not for you to know the times or dates the Father has set by his own authority. But you will receive power when the Holy Spirit comes on you; and you will be my witnesses *in Jerusalem, and in all Judea and Samaria,* and to the ends of the earth.' (Acts 1:7–8, my italics)

The disciples had been eager to find out what the 'next step' was going to be and they were probably wondering what their own role would be in the restoration of the kingdom to Israel. Would they be given positions of prominence and importance? What responsibilities would they have and what would their new level of authority be? The mechanics of the 'next step' and how they would fit into its implementation had become their chief focus, rather than the way of the cross, the only true path of discipleship. So Jesus answers them quite directly, saying in effect, 'That's just none of your business.'

The 'next step' may be the thing that we desire more than anything else in church leadership and in particular the role that we will play in causing that step to be taken, but more often than not we only discover the 'next step' when we're actually taking it! The Holy Spirit does this so that we have less opportunity to take the credit for what is about to take place in the life of the church. But the promise of God's power to *take* that step, through the anointing of the Holy Spirit, is as true today as it was then. Unfortunately those who were together on the evening he spoke to them after his resurrection didn't fully understand the need for a broken

and contrite heart to be in place before the river of the Holy
Spirit would not just *rest* upon them but *flow through them*
in power. In all the confusion and uncertainty that clouded
their thinking in those days immediately after Jesus' death
and resurrection they certainly hadn't understood the full
significance of what Jesus had said to them. The receipt of
'power to be witnesses' was entirely dependent on their absolute brokenness.

They may have thought at that time, 'We couldn't be any
more broken than we are right now – just look at what's happened to us over the last few days!' Perhaps that is why Jesus
didn't mention the need for more brokenness before there
could be the fulfilment of his word to them. But greater brokenness was the requirement for the 'next step', before the
gospel could be preached in Samaria and Judea in the power
of the Holy Spirit. They simply had no concept of the personal cost that was involved in their commissioning; that
almost all of them would be required to embrace a very
public death in front of the crowd at the hands of those who
hated their Master. If they were dreaming of a commission
from Jesus that would increase their authority in the world
as his kingdom was established they had failed to see how
this glorious acceleration into the kingdom would come
about. There was the need for even more brokenness before
they could be used in the way the Father wanted to use them.
And the Holy Spirit is still looking for broken vessels to pour
through into a needy world today.

The sluice gates are open!

Our willingness to be broken is an important key for God to
be able to open the sluice gate in our hearts that releases his
power to the multitudes in the valley. It was only through bro-

kenness that God was able to open the sluice gates in so many hearts following Stephen's death that a torrent of living water poured into the valley of decision, and first a city, then a region and then a nation were swept along by its power. The church was first broken and then built again in God's way, the region was impacted, and finally a distant country heard the good news of Jesus Christ from the lips of a new convert!

That would probably not have been the way we would have planned it, and had we been consulted about this 'next step' we would undoubtedly have raised numerous objections to it. It was certainly not in the mind of the early church on the day that Stephen's body lay battered and broken on the ground in front of a raging, hostile mob. But to God it was the perfect way: his church being built by a broken people through whom he was free to flow in astounding power. God is still looking for men and women who will humbly submit to his will for their lives whatever the cost and pain involved, and who will obey his commands to the letter in order to see his kingdom established.

LIFE APPLICATION

When you read about the lives of great men and women of God like Smith Wigglesworth, John Wesley or Amy Semple McPherson and imagine yourself in their position, what do your thoughts dwell on? The miracles and the mass salvations? Or the quality of their lives that made such events possible?

How does your 'ability in God' affect your humility?

PRAYER

Lord Jesus, today I make myself willing to be broken for your sake and for the sake of the lost. I know that without brokenness and humility you cannot do what you long to do with me. I ask you to put to death every fleshly thought that threatens to rob me of my inheritance in you and your ability to use me. Help me not to count the cost but to willingly lay down my life as a living sacrifice for your sake. Amen.

Rebuilding

6

Honour

Honour your father and your mother, as the LORD your God has commanded you, so that you may live long and that it may go well with you in the land the LORD your God is giving you.

Deuteronomy 5:16

From the top of Shadon's Hill you can see for miles, at least you can whenever our north-eastern weather permits it! From that vantage point you can look out over the major conurbation that makes up the county of Tyne and Wear, the home to over one million people that constitutes just one part of our harvest field. And just a few miles further on, lying behind some higher ground, live the rest of the three million people that God has entrusted to us to pastor.

After my encounter with Cesar Castellanos I found myself beginning to think about these people more and more often. Three million people who needed Jesus in their lives if they were not going to go to hell. Three million people still held in captivity by the devil and yet completely unaware of their predicament. Three million people that the church had largely failed to reach through an unwillingness to risk personal discomfort. They represented the 'multitudes in the valley of decision' that were our responsibility; the field that God had given to us to care for and from which we were to gather in a fruitful harvest. And yet most of our three million people weren't even aware that they had such an important and life-changing decision to make because the church had been so reticent in its proclamation and demonstration of the gospel. But the Holy Spirit was beginning to change our hearts, removing the offence that had been stored there, and opening the sluice gates that would in time allow the power of the gospel to change our region.

Clearly there was still a long way for us to go before a transformation of that magnitude could take place effectively, but God had begun the demolition process, had laid the new foundations in our hearts and was now beginning to build with us again, this time using new materials. Some of these materials were unfamiliar to us and produced some initial alarm; others were more familiar but had been de-emphasised or devalued in our previous style of leadership and needed to be reinstated.

Pastoring the region

One of the most important issues that we had to face up to as a church was the fact that we were personally responsible for the state of spiritual malnutrition and starvation found among those three million souls in our region. Along with the other congregations representing the many denominations that make up the body of Christ we had been given the responsibility of pastoring these people and feeding them with the word of life. The truth was, we had not been doing that very well at all and as a result the people in our region were starving to death for want of spiritual food. Starving people will eat anything, even things that will result in sickness and premature death, in order to satisfy their immediate hunger. When the city of Samaria was besieged by

Ben-Hadad, King of Aram, it wasn't long before the
people's hunger led to some desperate measures being taken:

> Some time later, Ben-Hadad king of Aram mobilised his entire
> army and marched up and laid siege to Samaria. There was a
> great famine in the city; the siege lasted so long that a donkey's
> head sold for eighty shekels of silver, and a quarter of a cab of
> seed pods for five shekels. (2 Kings 6:24–25)

Soon after this the people even resorted to cooking and
eating their own children, such was their intense hunger and
total desperation. Their predicament may have been due
largely to their own rebellion, but it was still the responsibility of Elisha, the man of God, to deliver them from their situation and provide them with access to wholesome food
once again through miraculous and divine intervention.

Of course, the moral condition of our region was the
result of a combination of factors. General rebellion against
the law of God among the people at large was one cause of
their starvation but our inactivity and inability as the church
to feed the people the Bread of Life was an equally important factor. The former we could 'only' pray about – but were
we praying? Or were we merely wringing our hands, lament-
ing the state of our society and hoping we could hang on
until Jesus returned without becoming contaminated by the
evil in the world all around us? As for feeding the starving,
well, we were happy to do that on the condition they all
humbled themselves and turned up at the right time each
Sunday morning to receive their rations for the week.

The sickness we were seeing in our society was actually
only the reflection of the diet of corruption that had of
necessity become their daily bread. The battle for their souls
now had to be fought on two fronts. First, and most obvious,
we needed to regain and take seriously Jesus' command to

preach the gospel. We had been reasonably good at pro-
claiming the gospel, having gained a lot of experience
preaching to the same saved people that came to church each
week, but we had little or no experience of demonstrating
the power of the gospel. We needed to rediscover the power
of proclamation *and* demonstration of the gospel to those
who really needed to hear it.

But second, and perhaps even more immediately, we
needed to undo some of the damage that the devil had
caused in the church by sowing his tares among the good
seed that was growing in our hearts. Unless these could be
dealt with we would only perpetuate the aberrations that had
'capped' our harvest in the past, preventing the Holy Spirit
from bringing the fruitfulness and multiplication that he had
been looking for for so long. One of the 'heart conditions'
that needed to be corrected at an early stage came as quite a
surprise to many of us. Almost immediately on our return
from the conference where we had first met Pastor
Castellanos, the Holy Spirit showed us a principle that, if
ignored, would stand in the way of God's ability to bless the
church, and through the church, the people of our region
and our nation.

Jesus could do no mighty work there . . .

Jesus had been amazing the people throughout the region of
Galilee with the demonstration of God's unlimited power
that accompanied his ministry. He had raised their dead,
healed all their sick, cast out demons wherever he found
them, cleansed their lepers and preached the good news to
them with authority. He had demonstrated to the religious
leaders that religion was both futile and an offence to God,
and skilfully countered every argument they levelled at him

with the truth. The people were now flocking to him from miles around to be healed and he had begun to gain a reputation among rulers and commoners alike as a man who deserved to be taken notice of. But despite his apparent success, Jesus had yet to encounter the greatest area of opposition to his work, which was to be found in the most unlikely of places – in his hometown among his own family and friends.

> And when the Sabbath had come, He began to teach in the synagogue. And many hearing Him were astonished, saying, 'Where did this Man get these things?' And 'What wisdom is this which is given to Him, that such mighty works are performed by His hands! Is this not the carpenter, the Son of Mary and brother of James, Joses, Judas, and Simon? And are not His sisters here with us?' And they were offended at Him. But Jesus said to them, 'A prophet is not without honor except in his own country, among his own relatives, and in his own house.' Now He could do no mighty work there, except that He laid His hands on a few sick people and healed them. (Mark 6:2–5 NKJV)

In all of the Gospels, the work of Jesus was opposed most effectively and vigorously by none other than his own family and friends! Jesus had been given authority by his Father to perform the miracles that had become associated with his ministry in the region, but in his hometown his friends and family had more important matters to attend to than the healing of the sick and raising of the dead. They did not recognise his divine mandate to perform the miracles that they had heard about and they didn't much care for his authoritative and radical teaching style either. Their critical view of him and the offence that was growing in their hearts was given vent when they openly confronted him by questioning his right to try and do those same things among them. 'Where did this Man get these things? And what wisdom is this which is given to Him, that such mighty works are performed by His hands!' they asked indignantly (verse 2). What they were really asking was, 'Where does he get his authority to speak to us in that way? Who does he think he is, behaving like that? After all, we know his parents, and the sort of stock he comes from!'

Their questions were simply the outward evidence of an inward attitude of heart that was dishonouring to Jesus. Their familiarity with him and with his natural parents produced contempt for his authority and as a result 'He could do no mighty work there' (verse 5). The attitude of heart that caused such dishonouring of God-given authority was the one thing that prevented Jesus from doing the mighty works he longed to perform among them. And here was the lesson that we needed to learn again if we were to both proclaim and demonstrate the power of the gospel. The obstacle to Jesus performing mighty works among his own family today is exactly the same as it was then – our lack of honour for those with God-given authority.

A nation that dishonours authority

When we look at our nation and the way in which we conduct ourselves as a society we can immediately see that we are a people that dishonour our national leaders much more readily than we honour them. Criticism comes to our lips more swiftly than praise. We 'sit in the seat of mockers' (Psalm1:1) as we join together to laugh at the images of our leaders as they are portrayed in satirical television programmes or mocked on the radio. God's word instructs us to pray for those in authority over us so that our proclamation of the gospel may be effective (1 Timothy 2:1–2) and in particular to submit to God-given governmental authority (1 Peter 2:13). But all too often we ignore those commands, choosing instead to allow the influence of the world to dictate our response to our leaders as we join in with the dishonour that is heaped upon them.

The inevitable end result of this kind of attitude of heart is that our easy familiarity with dishonour produces a behaviour pattern that is dragged into the life of the church and is taken as being entirely normal and acceptable. When we adopt these values the same problem arises in our church as it did in Jesus' day: Jesus is unable to do any mighty work through our own dishonoured leaders. We wonder why God doesn't give us the harvest we long for, but fail to see the divine principle that will open the door to the harvest and produce revival within the church: the honouring of godly leadership.

Rebellion – repentance – restoration

When Joshua died God's people began to go through a depressing and repetitive cycle of rebellion, repentance and restoration. When the people rebelled, God withdrew his hand of blessing and protection from the nation and they were besieged by their enemies who devastated their promised inheritance and ruined their harvest (Judges 6:4). At other times God withheld the rain their crops needed and the nation was afflicted by widespread famine. Whenever the people repented and cried out to God he would raise up judges who would be honoured by the people as being the means of God's deliverance, and for as long as they ruled, the nation would be under the blessing and protection of God once again (Judges 2:18).

During one such cycle when the famine had reached a peak, Naomi and Elimelech decided to move to the land of Moab where they had heard that there was grain to eat. They gathered their belongings together, packed their bags and set out on a 50-mile journey to the land of Moab where they settled down. In doing this they demonstrated the ease with which God's people can completely miss the point of the lesson that he is trying to teach. The famine in the promised land was the consequence of the collective sin of the nation and only repentance would heal the land and allow their inheritance to be fruitful once again. When had God ever said to his people, 'Whenever there is a famine in the land just abandon your inheritance that I have given you to tend and look after, and go and live in the land of Moab'? When had God ever said, 'If you can't survive with my provision then why don't you go and ask some other god who may be less fussy about your behaviour and see if he will provide for you'? Naomi and Elimelech should have realised that the only way for them to have a fruitful inheritance was to repent along with the people of their nation, but instead they failed to confront the truth, preferring to run to the world for help rather than their Saviour.

Repent or join in with the world

The church in our nation has abandoned its inheritance. We have abandoned our harvest field given to us by God, preferring to work in the world's field reaping a harvest of carnal grain. We have compromised our beliefs in order to become 'more acceptable' in the eyes and ears of the world. Some have denied the Virgin Birth, the Resurrection of Jesus and the power of the Holy Spirit in the life of the believer. Some have called the miracles of Jesus 'stories' and 'allegories' designed to teach us 'deeper truths' but not to be taken literally. Many have stopped preaching salvation from hell because it offends our dwindling congregations and hell sounds a little fanciful anyway. We have abandoned the command of God to 'Be holy, because I am holy' (1 Peter 1:16) and have allowed the corrupting influence of the world to spread unchecked through the body like a virulent disease. And after all of this we wonder why God seems so distant, why our influence in society is so insignificant and why the media treat us with disdain and ridicule those brave enough to stand up for 'Christian values'.

The church has entered a time of famine because it has abandoned its inheritance and gone to live in the land of Moab rather than facing up to the truth, repenting of sin and calling on God for forgiveness and mercy. We cannot feed a starving world with the bread of Moab and expect them to be satisfied. If we try to do that they will soon look elsewhere, and rightly so! Only the Bread of Life will truly satisfy the hunger of the starving multitudes in the valley of decision. The church must repent and return to its inheritance.

Disaster strikes

For ten years Naomi stayed in the land of Moab, eating the bread of the world and giving only an occasional thought to the promised inheritance which she and her husband Elimelech had left far behind. But soon disaster struck Naomi's household as first Elimelech and then her two sons Mahlon and Kilion died, leaving her and her two daughters-in-law to fend for themselves. The three women faced some tough decisions about their future and Naomi decided it was time to go back to Bethlehem where, she had heard, the

famine had come to an end. So she told Ruth and Orpah of
her decision and encouraged them to stay behind and find
new husbands and a new life in Moab while she got herself
ready to make another 50-mile journey back to Bethlehem
and her abandoned inheritance.

Now here is the same principle that the Holy Spirit wants
to draw to our attention once again. God always begins the
process of bringing us back to our inheritance by putting
some things to death. While their husbands were alive, had
Naomi ever attempted to return to her inheritance? No, she
had not. Had Elimelech ever made the decision to leave the
land of Moab and return to the land that God had given
him and the field that had been entrusted to him? No, he had
not. If he had thought about making the decision to return
home at any time it had certainly never been implemented,
because Naomi and her two daughters-in-law were all still
living comfortably in Moab when each of their husbands
died. It wasn't until they had *all* died that Naomi really
thought seriously about returning. This must have been a
very painful time for them all. When the husbands of
Naomi, Ruth and Orpah died, their security, future, liveli-
hood and provision died with them. But that point of desperation became the necessary stimulus for Naomi to move
back to her inheritance in God. Some things, even some
good things, have to die before we can start to return to our
field and our responsibility to reap the harvest God has been
preparing for us.

Jesus spelled this out more clearly to his disciples when he
said:

'Truly, truly, I say to you, unless a grain of wheat falls into
the earth and dies, it remains by itself alone; but if it dies, it
bears much fruit.' He who loves his life loses it; and he who

hates his life in this world shall keep it to life eternal. (John 12:24–25 NASB)

As disciples, our fruitfulness, and the fruitfulness of our field, depends upon our willingness to die to everything we hold most dear, even our very life itself! It is amazing how readily we gloss over those verses – or perhaps it isn't. The truth contained here is too uncomfortable for most of us to even begin to think about, let alone ask for it to be applied to our lives. But there are no grade A and grade B disciples, where grade B disciples are allowed to live a less strict life-style with less demanding entry criteria. There are just those who are disciples and those who are not.

The start of the journey home

Both Ruth and Orpah were encouraged by Naomi to go back to their families and start their lives over again. And both of them had the same opportunity to stay with Naomi if that was what they chose to do. Despite Orpah's genuine tears she chose to stay in the land of Moab, while Ruth pleaded with Naomi to let her return to Bethlehem with her.

> But Ruth replied, 'Don't urge me to leave you or to turn back from you. Where you go I will go, and where you stay I will stay. Your people will be my people and your God my God. Where you die I will die, and there I will be buried. May the LORD deal with me, be it ever so severely, if anything but death separates you and me.' (Ruth 1:16–17)

What was Ruth really saying? What had taken place in her heart to make her plead with Naomi like that? After all,

Ruth had no guarantees given to her by Naomi. There was no position being offered to her, no promise of an easy life or job security and, as a foreigner, no real likelihood of her getting remarried and having a family of her own. But Ruth recognised that, fragmented as it was, Naomi was the head of her family, and she was going to honour her for that.

She was in effect saying:

- I love you.
- I respect you.
- I trust you.
- I want to obey you.
- I am committed to staying with you.
- I am willing to serve you.

The principle of honour is far more than the mere recitation of words. It begins first in our heart before it comes out of our mouth and is demonstrated through a change in our actions. Ruth had made a decision in her heart that was to change the whole course of her life from there on. As we make the decision to honour our spiritual leaders we open the door of our heart to a measure of fruitfulness we have not previously experienced and a change of life and lifestyle that will alter us irrevocably.

Back home again

When they arrived in Bethlehem after their long journey they saw that the barley harvest had already begun and so Ruth said to Naomi: 'Let *me* go to the fields and pick up the leftover grain behind anyone in whose eyes I find favour.' Naomi said to her, 'Go ahead, my daughter' (Ruth 2:2, my italics).

Gleaning was hard work! Hour upon hour of back-breaking work in the hot sun gathering the few grains of barley dropped by the owner of the field's hired workers. And the local amenities weren't up to much either! There was no water provided for you to drink if you weren't an employee, and no shelter to sit in out of the burning heat of the noonday sun. As a single woman without the protection of friends around her there was always the risk of being molested by the other workers who might want some distraction from their hard labour in the field. This can't have come as a surprise to Ruth and yet despite knowing all this she said to Naomi, 'Let *me* go to the fields . . .' (Ruth 2:2). She did not say, 'Come on, Naomi, you got us into this mess, now pull your weight and help me do some work in the field or we're going to starve to death.'

Ruth was saying:

- Because I love you . . .
- Because I respect you . . .
- Because I trust you . . .
- Because I am committed to staying with you . . .
- I am willing to serve you by working hard in the harvest field.

Can we say the same? As we look at our church and the men and women God has anointed to lead us do we find it easier to blame them for 'the mess *they* have got us into'? Or do we, like Ruth, say to them, 'Because I love you and respect you, because I trust you and am committed to staying with you, I am willing to serve you wholeheartedly by personally working hard in the harvest field'? Our response will determine the size of our harvest.

It was with that committed and willing attitude of heart that Ruth left for the field that belonged to Boaz where she discovered the power of this principle in action.

Honour is attractive and releases the harvest

Ruth was soon noticed by the owner of the field, Boaz, who proceeded to ask his foreman who she was and why she was gleaning in his field. The foreman told Boaz everything he knew about her and how she was working for her mother-in-law Naomi, and on hearing this Boaz decided to have mercy on her. He offered her free access to the water that had been drawn by his men for the hired workers to drink, a place to sit in the shade and rest when she got tired, and some of their food to eat when they broke for lunch. In addition he instructed his workers to drop some of their stalks of barley so she could have more to pick up.

Ruth was amazed by his kindness and asked him directly why he was being so generous towards her:

'Why have I found such favour in your eyes that you notice me – a foreigner?' Boaz replied, 'I've been told all about what you have done for your mother-in-law since the death of your husband – how you left your father and mother and your homeland and came to live with a people you did not know before. May the LORD repay you for what you have done. May you be richly rewarded by the LORD, the God of Israel, under whose wings you have come to take refuge.' (Ruth 2:10–12)

The one thing that impressed Boaz over every other attribute she may have possessed was the honour that Ruth showed for Naomi and which was demonstrated by her willingness to serve her by working hard in the harvest field.

She was not simply doing this for herself; she was doing it on behalf of Naomi whom she loved, trusted, respected and honoured! Her reward for this honour was a larger than expected harvest at the end of the day. Imagine Naomi's surprise when Ruth turned up that evening after a hard day's work in the field, expecting her to have gathered enough grain to prepare a little gruel to eat before they went to bed, but instead of a small handful of grain Ruth staggered in carrying a 50 kg sack of threshed grain and some of her leftover lunch to share with Naomi (Ruth 2:17–18)! This was a far greater harvest than either of them had expected! And what had made that abundant harvest possible? The honour that she had shown to the owner of the field for her mother-in-law, Naomi.

Honour releases the harvest

The key that opened the door to the harvest was the honour that Ruth gave to Naomi, the head of her family. One of the most frequently quoted Bible verses in our churches is found in Matthew 9 where Jesus says to his disciples: 'The harvest is plentiful but the workers are few. Ask the Lord of the harvest, therefore, to send out workers into his harvest field' (Matthew 9:37–38).

We may be tempted to use this verse to thrash ourselves over the head in order to make ourselves (or our congregation) feel even more guilty about our lack of fruitfulness or in an effort to spur us on into some increased 'activity' in evangelism. Or we may simply use it as a means of attempting to justify biblically our inability to gather a harvest because we 'haven't got the right workers'. But what will enable the Lord of the great harvest that we long to see gathered in, to send out his labourers into the harvest field and release a bigger harvest of souls than we ever believed possible? The honour we show to our leadership. And who will the labourers be? We will!

The perversion of honour

Honour is a concept perverted by Satan for very obvious reasons! If the honouring of godly leadership releases the harvest of souls then honour is something he will actively attempt to discredit, and dishonour is something he will do his best to promote. We have seen already that when the church abandons its inheritance it opens the back door to the influence of the world with its values then being dictated and determined by the prince of this world (John 16:11). With dishonour running rife throughout the church the prospect of abundant harvest is made ever more unlikely, much to his relief.

Honour has actually become a dirty word. Whenever someone begins to talk about honour we turn our nose up at them because we have a perverted understanding of what the word really means. To many honour implies a sickening, boot-licking, crawling posture adopted by social climbers who want to ingratiate themselves in the eyes of those who have real power. They see the person being honoured in this way as a dictatorial power-mad despot whose only goal in life is to control lesser mortals like themselves and tell them what they should and shouldn't be doing. Perhaps this is something of a caricature of the real situation, but we can probably all identify with the negative feelings we experience when we think of honouring our leaders, spiritual or otherwise. If this is our concept of honour then we need to ask the Holy Spirit to transform our perverted understanding by the renewing of our minds.

Do not conform any longer to the pattern of this world, but be transformed by the renewing of your mind. Then you will be able to test and approve what God's will is – his good, pleasing and perfect will. (Romans 12:2)

Our worldly value-systems and thought patterns need to be transformed by the power of the Spirit so we can understand the good, pleasing and perfect will of God for his church. Ruth's honouring of Naomi was very straightforward and ours should be no different. We ought to be able to look to those whom God has placed with leadership responsibility over us in the church and say to them:

- I love you.
- I respect you.
- I trust you.
- I want to obey you.
- I am committed to staying with you.
- And I am willing to serve you *by working hard in the harvest field.*

If we can't say that to our leaders, then why are we in their church?

The result of honour is abundant harvest

Finally, if we follow the progress of Ruth through the four chapters that tell her story we see an amazing pattern developing that should be an encouragement to each of us as we consider the size of the harvest that needs to be brought in.

In Chapter 1

Ruth has nothing. Everything of personal value has died and she is in a desperate and uncertain position. But even in that position she chooses to honour the head of her family, Naomi, and covenants to stay with her whatever the future holds. Having nothing or having lost everything of value is no reason for dishonouring God's chosen leaders. This is the first step towards reaping a great harvest.

In Chapter 2

Ruth honours Naomi by offering to personally work in the harvest field. Her expectation is low – she does not expect to see much in the way of results by the end of the day. But in honouring the head of her family she catches the eye of the lord of the harvest, Boaz, who allows her to return home with 50 kg of grain that she has gleaned from the field. As we honour our leaders, despite all their imperfections and failures, we will begin to reap a surprisingly large harvest of souls. Isn't that what we want?

In Chapter 3

Ruth continues to honour Naomi by obeying her instructions regarding Boaz (Ruth 3:5–6). Her reward on this occasion was to receive six large measures of threshed grain directly from Boaz, who poured them into her shawl and lifted the heavy load onto her shoulders to take away (Ruth 3:15). The lord of the harvest was now personally supervising her 'work' and blessing her with even more than she believed possible. Persistent honour brings increased blessing from the owner of the field.

In Chapter 4

Ruth now honours Naomi's wishes *and* the lord of the harvest, Boaz, by marrying him. Honouring godly leaders results in the possibility of greater intimacy with the lord of the harvest. And now she no longer has to glean the field –

she *owns the whole field*! If we want to own the 'whole field' of our region or our city, what must we do to make this happen? The answer is clear: honour those leaders God has placed over us and offer to work hard in the harvest field on their behalf.

Reconciliation and the church

It doesn't require the efforts of a highly proficient market research company to see that the church is not perfect, nor are its leaders. Disagreements between the leadership and the members of the church often produce acrimonious church splits where both the leadership and the members become seriously injured, nursing their wounds as they painfully limp to their new church 'just down the road'. Transfer growth in this situation is often nothing more than rearranging the deck chairs on a sinking ship. What is really needed is reconciliation between the wounded members and their equally wounded leadership.

Paul says: 'And he has committed to us the message of reconciliation' (2 Corinthians 5:19). Before we can proclaim the message of reconciliation to the world we must see it at work within Christ's body, the church. Over the course of time, as we taught this principle to the church, we met with many people who came to repent of their 'attitudes' towards us as leaders. And it was not all one-sided. We, too, had to repent of the hurts that we had caused as leaders of the church to members past and present. But soon we were hearing of people who had joined our church from other churches returning to their previous leaders and repenting of their attitude of dishonour toward them which had been at least in part responsible for their lack of fruitfulness and genuine growth as a church. The results have been impressive. The number of souls being saved has increased as the wounds of the past have been healed. We were excited at the power of this principle that the Holy Spirit was teaching us and it made us eager to learn even more.

LIFE APPLICATION

1. How many people have I led to Christ in the last six months? A few grains? A handful? Or a 50 kg sack of grain?
2. What has been my attitude to the leader(s) of my church? Have I honoured them in the way I should?
3. Humility and repentance are necessary prerequisites to restoration of the harvest by God. Are there any leaders past or present to whom I need to repent about dishonouring them? Have I been the unwitting cause of them being unable to see a mighty work in their church?

PRAYER

Father, forgive me for dishonouring your servants [name]. I confess my sin to you now. In particular I ask you to forgive me for [be specific]. Please give me the courage to contact them and repent. I ask you to bless them in their ministry. Make them prosperous, protect them from all harm and bring peace to their family. I ask this for the sake of the harvest that you are preparing to have gathered in. In Jesus' name. Amen.

7

Encountering God

Then the man said, 'Your name will no longer be Jacob, but Israel, because you have struggled with God and with men and have overcome.'

Genesis 32:28

They just seemed to be completely beyond reach. Everything he had tried to do or say to communicate his love for God and God's love for them seemed to have had little or no impact on their lives. Even when they had told him about a problem they were facing and he had offered to pray for them their response had been dismissive: 'OK, *you* can pray for us but *we'll* sort it out for ourselves.' When their problem was resolved more quickly than they had expected, they didn't call in to express their thanks for the prayers that had been offered on their behalf, and when he reminded them that he had been praying for them, they were unwilling to see the connection between his prayers and the successful resolution of their problem. It was really quite discouraging.

One evening he returned home after a busy day at work and walked out into his back garden. There, looking over the fence that separated the two properties, was his neighbour. He seemed to have been waiting for him to come outside, so he asked him how things were going. He expected the usual courteous superficiality that had, up to that time, character-ised their relationship as neighbours, but instead was sur-prised at the candour of the reply. 'We're pretty devastated,' he said. 'We've just come back from the doctor and he had some very bad news for us. My wife's been unwell for some time and the doctor did some investigations and they have found a growth. We don't know whether it's cancer or not and he's going to arrange some further tests to try and find out what's causing it.' This was the most open and vulnerable expression of reality that he had ever heard from his neighbour and his heart was moved with compassion for them both.

'That's dreadful news,' he said, 'But I believe Jesus can heal sick bodies, and I believe it because I saw it happen when my own mother was healed from multiple sclerosis. One day she was suffering with it; she went to church and was prayed for, and she went home completely healed. If you would like I'll pray for your wife that Jesus will heal her in the same way as he healed my mother.' He half expected the same kind of negative response that he had heard in the past whenever he mentioned Jesus' name, but instead he heard his neighbour say, 'Thank you, I'll go and get her right now.'

After a few moments the neighbour returned with his wife and they stood together against the fence. He explained to them both that he was going to lay his hand on her in line with the teaching found in the Bible and ask that Jesus would heal her completely. He leant over the fence and stretched out his hand to touch her on the shoulder and prayed that Jesus would heal her, whatever the cause of her sickness. They thanked him and after a few moments went back inside their house very obviously moved by what had just taken place. A few days later he saw them again, but this time there were no barriers to overcome. The investigations had come back and there was no trace of the malignancy that they had so feared. 'Thank you so much for praying for me!' she said, and her husband joined in enthusiastically, 'I know it made all the difference.'

What does *he* really want?

When my friend first told me that story the Holy Spirit began to speak to me about our attitude towards the love of God. The Bible teaches us that the Father is actively looking for worshippers who can be intimate with him (John 4:23) and who can express their love from whole hearts, hearts that have been cleansed from all trace of sin and independence of spirit. The Holy Spirit also longs for intimacy with us because he is the one who makes that intimate worship with the Father possible (Philippians 3:3). Unfortunately we are often less than willing to worship God in that way. We want intimacy with the Father, but only on our terms and according to the conditions that we lay down, which usually have more to do with our need for personal recognition and approval than the unmerited favour of the grace of God at work in our lives. We prefer to substitute activity for adoration and work for worship, believing quite mistakenly that this is the only way that we can truly be appreciated by him, and thereby gain that favoured position by his side. We reason, 'If only he can see how hard we are trying to please him he will surely see how much *we* are worth,' when in reality he wants us to see how much *he* is worth.

Of course, when we do this we completely bypass the work of the cross of Christ. Denying his power to forgive and heal the worst of sinners, we fail to recognise that in ourselves we really have nothing of worth that would make us at all appealing to God outside of Jesus. And worse than this, we unwittingly build a fence that keeps us distant from the one we say we love and that produces an attitude of heart very similar to that of the neighbour in the story who was dismissive of any move my friend made to draw closer to him. We say to God as he approaches us, 'By all means, *you* go and get on with the job of saving the world, but *we'll* get on with the real business of building the church. There are wages to be paid, buildings to maintain, people to see, sermons to preach, plans to discuss, prayers to be prayed, programmes to administer and we don't have very much time for anything else. But at least you can see how much we love you – just look at all the things we're doing!' Each time we respond to his advances like this we are merely reasserting our desire for independence from him, our resistance to his call to walk with us as lovers and our unwillingness to let him get involved with an area of our life that we consider to be 'our own business' and not his.

And yet despite this the Father still extends a hand of friendship and love toward us. His heart burns with an intense longing to reach out to us and heal us, to touch our wounded spirits and make us whole. But he cannot do that until we are willing to open up our hearts to him, laying down our pride and allowing ourselves to become vulnerable before him. Our busy-ness and self-sufficiency only become a barrier that prevents us from being intimate with him in the way that he longs to be. And in the church the biggest barriers are often found at leadership level. As leaders we talk to our church about the need for intimacy with God and sincerely believe that we are having the kind of fellowship with him that he wants to have with us. When challenged we point to the evidence of our work for him as the main indicator of our intimacy, when more often than not we are really living behind our fence, forcing him to keep his distance, quite unable to reach over and heal our wounded spirits.

Am I doing OK?

The crowd came to Jesus one day and asked, 'What must we do to do the works God requires?' (John 6:28).

'How will we know if we're working hard enough for God?' they were asking. 'What sort of things can we do to make him really appreciate us?'

Jesus' answer took them as much by surprise then as it does many of us today: Jesus answered, 'The work of God is this: to believe in the one he has sent' (John 6:29).

The 'work' that pleases God is this: having intimate fellowship with his Son. Pleasing God does not come through our own hard work and accomplishments but by having a close and loving relationship with Jesus through the power of the Spirit. Intimacy and independence are like light and darkness: they cannot exist together. Our Father longs for the intimacy of worshippers who will worship him in spirit and in truth and who will really appreciate *his* worth in the way that true 'worth-ship' requires. But our independence cries out for some other means, any other means, of demonstrating *our* value and worth to him. God is longing to reach over that fence to touch us, to share his whole heart and life with us, but he waits for us to invite him to draw close. He is waiting for any opportunity that would make this level of intimacy possible. And if the opportunity doesn't seem to occur naturally – then he is willing to create one!

Marinade or meat hammer?

I am no cook. The finer points of cordon bleu or nouveau cuisine are lost on me. But I do know that there is more than one way to tenderise meat. Meat can be marinated, soaked in wine, vinegar, oils and spices to tenderise it and prepare it for cooking, or it can be beaten with a meat hammer. Whichever method is used the chef's desire is to get that tough meat thoroughly tender so it can be enjoyed by everyone in the way he wants it to be enjoyed. The Holy Spirit can use the marinating approach, gently soaking our hearts and tenderising them so that we willingly allow him to draw near. At other times he has to use the meat hammer.

Devastating problems and difficulties can sometimes be the only means by which the Holy Spirit can gain access to previously fenced-off parts of our lives. Just like my friend's neighbour in the story, when faced with such painful situations in life we are more inclined to walk up to the fence and allow him to reach over and touch us. And while we might prefer to apply this principle exclusively to someone encountering God for the first time, the Holy Spirit uses this same method throughout our Christian life to ensure ongoing intimate contact that will produce healthy growth in our relationship with him. His goal is to destroy the fence altogether because it represents our independence from him, but he begins by reaching over the fence and touching our hearts. The Holy Spirit is committed to seeing people become tender-hearted towards him, because they are the only kind of people he can use to build his church. Hard hearts can't be intimate with Jesus, preferring to take refuge behind a fence of their own making.

'You can have your church back!'

During the early months of the renewal that came to Sunderland in late 1994 the Holy Spirit began to use both the marinade and the meat hammer to revive his church throughout the region. Some evenings we would be overwhelmed by the gentle presence of the Holy Spirit who would speak tenderly to us and reassure us of the Father's love for us as we lay on the floor doing 'carpet time'. On other evenings he was not so gentle! I well remember one of those early meetings where the Holy Spirit had been saying very clearly that the Father wanted to break the controlling hands of church leadership from their stranglehold on the church, because he wanted his church back. One of the pastors from a church in the region who was, until that evening, rather sceptical about what had been going on in these meetings, made a move to come forward for prayer. Suddenly, and quite without warning, the Holy Spirit picked him up off his feet and threw him backwards, sending him crashing through several rows of chairs before depositing him rather roughly on the ground amid the wreckage. When we talked to him afterwards about what had taken place that evening he said, 'When that happened I thought, "Well, God, if you're going to be that violent about it you can have your church back!"'

We came to realise that whatever approach the Holy Spirit took, gentle or not so gentle, he knew the best way of dealing with the issues of our heart that were keeping us at a distance from him. We were coming to appreciate that if we really wanted to encounter God then we must be ready to encounter him on his terms, and we had no right to stipulate the conditions or the manner in which that encounter took place.

Called to be followers of Christ

The methods used to call the apostles Peter and Paul typify the two approaches the Holy Spirit uses to draw followers of Jesus into the life of intimacy. Both Peter and Paul encountered God in a life-changing way. Both went on to be major figures in the early church and both experienced the power of God at work in their lives and flowing out through them into the community in extraordinary ways. But they each encountered God in a very different manner. Peter was a fisherman who, along with his brother Andrew, had quite a successful fishing business in the seaside town of Bethsaida near Capernaum. His first encounter with the Holy Spirit came long before he met with Jesus through the ministry of John the Baptist, who as the forerunner of the Messiah preached a baptism of repentance for the forgiveness of sins (Luke 3:3).

Every level of society was touched by John's preaching and teaching, including Peter and his brother, and it wasn't long before John began to disciple those convicted by the Holy Spirit of their need for more of God and less of themselves. Those who submitted to this baptism had hearts that were prepared to receive the Messiah when he came. The ground of their hearts had already been thoroughly ploughed through John's discipling and many of the thorns that had been growing in their hearts had been torn out so that Jesus' words had no difficulty taking root and producing a great harvest:

> All the people, even the tax collectors, *when they heard Jesus' words*, acknowledged that God's way was right, *because they had been baptised by John*. But the Pharisees and experts in the law rejected God's purpose for themselves, *because they had not been baptised by John*. (Luke 7:29–30, my italics)

As a disciple of John the Baptist (John 1:35–42) Peter was already familiar with the cost of discipleship and the need for personal repentance in order to prepare the way for the coming Messiah. Because the ground of his heart had already been prepared Peter could respond immediately when Jesus called him to be one of his disciples: '"Come, follow me," Jesus said, "and I will make you fishers of men." *At once* they left their nets and followed him' (Mark 1:17–18, my italics).

There was no need for a violent physical shaking or a life-threatening crisis in order for Peter to obey Jesus' command. True, there still remained some 'fences' in Peter's life that acted as barriers to the intimacy that Jesus required. These were the seeds of worldliness that threatened to re-cultivate the ground that had been ploughed by John's ministry, not least of which was the security of his occupation and the comfortable way of life that, along with his brother Andrew, he enjoyed. But these were not deep-rooted thorns with years of growth to add to their strength, nor had they yet grown to form an impenetrable fence for Jesus to overcome when he called him. Jesus needed only to show Peter his complete authority over his personal fears by providing him with the biggest catch of fish he had ever seen, a catch so great that it threatened to swamp the boat. That act alone was enough to convince Peter of two things: his own sinfulness in the presence of his Messiah and the privilege of being asked to be a follower of Jesus (Luke 5:8). The necessary 'next step' that took him from being a follower of John to becoming a follower of Jesus was more of a gentle progression than a violent leap. The Holy Spirit had been using the marinating approach for some time in order to draw Peter into intimacy and he did not need to use the meat hammer method by bringing him to a crisis point in his life before he got the response he was looking for. It is interesting to note that a few years later, after Judas's death, when the apostles met together to prayerfully consider a replacement for him, it was Peter under the anointing of the Holy Spirit who stipulated the qualifications required for such a man:

'For,' said Peter, 'it is written in the Book of Psalms, "May his place be deserted; let there be no-one to dwell in it," and, "May another take his place of leadership." Therefore it is necessary to choose one of the men who have been with us the whole time the Lord Jesus went in and out among us, *beginning from John's baptism* to the time when Jesus was taken up from us. For one of these must become a witness with us of his resurrection.' (Acts 1:20–22, my italics)

Matthias, who was chosen as Judas's replacement, was a man who had been through the same preparatory process of Holy Spirit 'marinating' as Peter and whose 'promotion' would be understood for what it really was – complete surrender to the life of the cross through whole-hearted discipleship.

Paul encounters the meat hammer!

The Holy Spirit's dealing with the apostle Paul, however, was a rather different matter. The religious bigot known as Saul, steeped in years of proud tradition and the dry ritualistic 'worship' of God, needed a much more direct and even violent approach to bring him to the point of willing obedience and intimacy. The ground of his heart was little more than the well-trodden path of traditional, ritualistic worship and it needed to be broken up before the seed could be sown, and in time harvested effectively.

As he neared Damascus on his journey, suddenly a light from heaven flashed around him. He fell to the ground and heard a voice say to him, 'Saul, Saul, why do you persecute me?' 'Who are you, Lord?' Saul asked. 'I am Jesus, whom you are persecuting,' he replied. 'Now get up and go into the city, and you will be told what you must do.' The men travelling with Saul stood there speechless; they heard the sound but did not see anyone. Saul got up from the ground, but when he opened his eyes he could see nothing. So they led him by the hand into Damascus. For three days he was blind, and did not eat or drink anything. (Acts 9:3–9)

Imagine how desperate Saul must have felt encountering the One he had been persecuting so zealously, quite convinced that this Jesus was a religious aberration and not a real person any more. Put yourself in Saul's shoes for a moment and consider how you would have felt if you were suddenly overwhelmed by a brilliant light that left you quite unable to see anything, and heard a voice that you didn't recognise speaking to you with great authority, the voice of someone who was obviously responsible for your injury but who gave you no guarantee that you would ever have your eyesight restored. And to make matters worse when you asked your travelling companions who had knocked you so violently to the ground, they could honestly say they hadn't seen anyone do anything. No wonder Saul suddenly lost his appetite! The Holy Spirit had chosen to use the meat hammer approach on this occasion – and it worked! Saul's pride and self-righteous confidence before God was dealt a death blow on that day through the violent work of the Holy Spirit as he tore open the ground of Saul's heart, ploughing up the hard soil of the path and sowing the seed of the heavenly vision in its place. The success of this work performed by the Holy Spirit was still evident in Paul's life many years later when he wrote to the Philippian church:

If anyone else thinks he has reasons to put confidence in the flesh, I have more: circumcised on the eighth day, of the people of Israel, of the tribe of Benjamin, a Hebrew of Hebrews; in regard to the law, a Pharisee; as for zeal, persecuting the church; as for legalistic righteousness, faultless. But whatever was to my profit I now consider loss for the sake of Christ. What is more,

I consider everything a loss compared to *the surpassing great-ness of knowing Christ Jesus my Lord*, for whose sake I have lost all things. I consider them rubbish, that I may gain Christ and be found in him, not having a righteousness of my own that comes from the law, but that which is through faith in Christ – the righteousness that comes from God and is by faith. *I want to know Christ* and the power of his resurrection and the fellow-ship of sharing in his sufferings, becoming like him in his death, and so, somehow, to attain to the resurrection from the dead. (Philippians 3:4–11, my italics)

Paul's chief concern was to know that life of intimacy with Jesus on a daily basis. The Greek word translated in this passage as 'to know' is *ginosko*, which is the same word used to describe the intimacy of sexual union in the context of marriage (Matthew 1:25; Luke 1:34). Such intimacy is per-sonal, exclusive, passionate and edifying to the relationship. While clearly not sexual in reference, after the Holy Spirit had dealt with Saul's fierce pride and independence Paul longed for this kind of personal, exclusive, passionate, edify-ing and intimate relationship with his Saviour with the same intensity as a bride longs for the groom (Ephesians 5:32). His other achievements, those things that had previously given him such security and had forged his identity when he was one of the crowd, were now entirely irrelevant in compari-son to the pleasure of encountering the One who had died for his sins. The meat hammer approach might have seemed unusually violent at the time, but there was no doubting its long-term beneficial effect.

Encountering God is a lifestyle – not an event

While recognising that the Holy Spirit often works decisively at a critical moment in a person's life in the way that we have read with both Peter and Paul, we also need to realise that these were not one-off events. Peter and Paul continually encountered the refining work of God in the person of the Holy Spirit throughout their whole life. In this way encountering God became a lifestyle rather than an event. The Holy Spirit constantly wanted to reach over any fences they had built, and having made contact with their heart, destroy that fence that kept them apart from him. The same is true for each one of us today. Healing weekends and deliverance sessions are important, but nothing can replace the transforming work of the Holy Spirit as he is encountered on a daily, moment by moment basis. Our challenge as church leaders was to encourage and facilitate our ongoing need for a daily encounter with the Holy Spirit in the lives of the whole church.

From the time that Lois and I met Cesar Castellanos at the Assembly of God conference we realised that our model of church needed to change. We began to introduce the concept of the cell church to our people and before too long had established cells that embraced most of our church congregation. These cells were not the 'end product' but a necessary transitional structure that would help take us from our traditional church model into a thoroughly cell-based church. Within these cells a certain amount of 'discipleship' was already beginning to take place and as a result there was an increasing fruitfulness both in the lives of those taking part in the cell and in an increasing number of people being saved. But the most exciting aspect of this change, and the second of the emphases that we introduced to the church, was to be found at the weekend events that we encouraged every member to attend. Beginning on Friday evening, continuing through all day Saturday and closing with the afternoon session immediately following on from the Sunday morning celebration, we gave ourselves to hear from the Holy Spirit and to allow him to minister to our hearts.

During these times, known as Encounter Weekends, the cross takes centre stage and we actively seek the revelation of the Holy Spirit regarding issues of personal sin, demonic strongholds and areas of oppression that lie hidden just beneath the surface in all of our lives. There is little or no personal directional input and no one-on-one counselling apart from that which the Holy Spirit brings to each individual. During the course of these sessions time is set aside to enable the Holy Spirit to expose areas of our lives where we are not healed, either emotionally or spiritually. Specific sins are identified and confronted by ticking them off on an explicit check list, and after acknowledging the price that Jesus paid on the cross to cleanse us from their corrupting power we bring this sheet to the cross, symbolically shredding our list in a paper shredder. In doing this we acknowledge that his blood is the only means possible of dealing with the injury caused to ourselves and to others through our sin. Demonic strongholds and areas of oppression in our lives are identified and addressed through deliverance and the fruit of this is evident in the lives of those who have been set free during these times.

Beginning with our existing leadership we systematically took the church through these encounter sessions. Amazing things began to happen. Sometimes the process the Holy Spirit used was a gentle marinating, and at other times it was a more violent hammering, but each time, and without exception, people were healed and set free from significant areas of control that Satan had had in their lives up to that point. People were sometimes devastated as the Holy Spirit unearthed something so well hidden that they had completely forgotten about it, but this was more than made up for by the healing that he brought once it had been taken to the cross and dealt with.

People publicly confessed sins to the group that had been submerged for years under the baggage and clutter of church life and day-to-day living. Childhood abuse was disclosed along with fears that had entered and taken up residence at that time. Dysfunctional parents were forgiven and honoured instead of being hated and dishonoured. Restitution and reconciliation began to take place throughout the church, spreading far beyond the small group that had met together that weekend, as forgiveness was sought from people with whom they had been in conflict for years. People went to pastors in the churches that they had previously attended and sought their forgiveness for dishonouring them and robbing them of their harvest. The leaders in turn asked their forgiveness for their past errors of leadership. And through all of this the hearts of God's people were being healed and the devil's influence was being broken. It was (and is) extremely painful, but it is also incredibly wonderful to be set free by Jesus.

But we realised that these weekends were just the start, and not the end, of a process that the Holy Spirit wanted us to become entirely familiar with. Encountering God was not to be an event – it was to be a lifestyle, and these weekends became a useful starting point from which to launch out into deeper water with the Holy Spirit on a daily basis.

LIFE APPLICATION

How much of your week has been taken up with the busyness of church activity? How much time has been spent with the Holy Spirit? Which has proved to be the most fruitful?

What are your 'terms and conditions' for intimacy with

Jesus? What fences have you erected that effectively keep him at arm's length? What are you willing to do about them?

PRAYER

Dear Holy Spirit, I ask you to reveal Jesus to me. I want to know you in the passionate, exclusive and intimate way that Paul desired. Help me to develop a lifestyle of encountering you, a process and not just an event in the day. I relinquish my personal 'terms and conditions' and ask that you apply yours to our relationship from now on. Amen.

8

Becoming a Follower

After Jesus had finished instructing his twelve disciples, he went on from there to teach and preach in the towns of Galilee.

Matthew 11:1

Recently I began to reflect on the years that Lois and I have worked together in the ministry. I recalled how very privileged we had been to meet many anointed Christian leaders who, out of our relationship with them, came and ministered at our church in Sunderland. I remembered how delighted we had been to act as hosts for them, and the pleasure we had received from being able to invite people from the region to visit our church and sit under their ministry, which was invariably significant in its timing in the life of the church. We appreciated their wisdom, born out of years of experience caring for God's people, and were very grateful for the input through the preaching and teaching of God's word that they brought to the church.

But in time, we found ourselves in the same position of potential influence in the life of the many churches we visited as we began to travel internationally, attending and speaking at conferences all around the world. I couldn't help but wonder what long-term impact, if any, our visit would have on the life of that local church. We knew that people were touched by the Holy Spirit in the conferences at which we spoke, but were unable to assess whether those meetings had any significant long-term impact on their lives or if they had simply enjoyed the experience without it producing a change in behaviour and a greater measure of personal holiness. Had the things we had preached taken root in their hearts and produced good fruit in their lives and in the life of the church, or had it been 'just another sermon' from just another itinerant minister? Perhaps that was something we would not be privileged to discover this side of eternity, but as I looked back over the years of meetings that I had personally attended I could remember many occasions where the Holy Spirit had impacted my life, challenged my complacency or required me to repent of sin, but oddly enough I could remember almost nothing of what the preacher had said on each of those occasions. It was almost as though the preacher had been acting as an agent employed by God to introduce me to the Holy Spirit and that once I had encountered the Holy Spirit, he became the most memorable part of that meeting. I had to ask myself why I thought it should be any different when I was the one delivering the word. And yet I couldn't help wondering whether the time I spent in preparation and the effort of delivering the burden that the Holy Spirit had entrusted to my heart actually resulted in many changed lives.

Preaching is important

One day I was talking to a friend who works as a family doctor about our apparent inability to retain most of the information we hear. He told me that it was his practice to ensure that whatever he had said to his patient during the consultation, whatever explanation he had given or illustration he had used, he would always try to save the most important piece of information (usually how to take the tablets!) until they were just about to leave the room. He reasoned that the last thing they heard was probably the *only* thing they would remember accurately, and that everything else would either be forgotten, misfiled or resemble the information conveyed at the end of a long line of Chinese whispers within a few seconds of having left the room. Perhaps this was an over-pessimistic view, but I couldn't help acknowledging that this did seem to be the case in many of our church meetings. How many of our church members took notes? Of those who did, how many revised them when they got home, asking the Holy Spirit to apply the word to their life that week? And by contrast, how many would you overhear at the end of a meeting quoting something to a fellow church member which they confidently attributed to your sermon that morning, which you most definitely had *not* said, involving a passage of Scripture that you hadn't even remotely thought about using, never mind included in your sermon? And how many would be quite unable to remember one word that had been spoken five minutes after they had left the church building?

Psychologists tell us that only 5–15 per cent of people listening to someone teaching them in a lecture room setting will actually take the information conveyed and apply it to their life. And yet despite this discovery the church has continued over many years to use this method as its main strategy for encouraging and promoting spiritual growth. As I thought about it I began to feel rather discouraged. If so little was retained and even less was applied, why did I spend so much time in prayer and study preparing for that word?

Before we become too discouraged we need to recognise the value that God places on preaching and teaching in the life of the believer, and its importance as a means of healthy growth and maturity in the church. Without it we could rightly be accused of living on the froth of experience rather than feeding on the meat of the word. The Bible teaches that the early church grew rapidly because the apostles dedicated themselves 'to prayer and the ministry of the word' (Acts 6:4, my italics). Healthy growth comes from a healthy diet and Jesus said that we require a diet that not only includes but relies predominantly on the word of God (Matthew 4:4). We are exhorted to 'fight the good fight of the faith' and so we have been given a lethal weapon, the 'sword of the Spirit, which is the word of God' (Ephesians 6:17) that requires the dexterity that comes through regular use to deliver great damage to the devil and all his works. We are told that we are made holy and cleansed by 'the washing with water through the word' (Ephesians 5:26), and that his word is constantly 'at work in [those] who believe' (1 Thessalonians 2:13).

Nevertheless, despite the importance of the word in our life, I couldn't help noticing that there were some people who *heard* the word repeatedly but didn't seem to *do* anything with it. And then there were those who seemed to have good hearing when I spoke to them before the service began who didn't seem to hear a single word of the sermon at all! James clearly noticed the same problem in the early church and summed the situation up when he challenged them by saying: 'Do not merely listen to the word, and so deceive yourselves. *Do what it says*' (James 1:22, emphasis mine).

Jesus gave us clear instruction on the importance of God's word when he declared that his family would be recognisable by their willingness to hear the word *and* put it into practice (Luke 8:21). He also said that anybody who heard his word and didn't put it into practice was a fool (Matthew 7:26). How then is it still possible that, after years of great sermons and excellent teaching in our churches, and with all these

warnings and exhortations to hear and apply the word liber-
ally scattered throughout Scripture, there is still such an
obstacle for us to overcome before the revelation of the word
of God is translated into action in our lives?

Preaching doesn't change the church!

As I considered this further, I began to realise that the
problem in the church seemed to be less the hearing of
the word and more the application of it. Less the 'fault' of
the preacher and more the failure to inculcate those things
that the Holy Spirit was saying. In order for the word to
change our lives we must first have the ability to hear it and
then have the means of applying it. It became apparent that
we needed to rediscover the fundamental principle taught by
Jesus: that preaching by itself will not change the church;
only discipleship will. Jesus did not command us to make
people who would be good listeners or great note-takers. He
called us to make disciples.

The reason for this should be obvious: however relevant
the sermon or anointed the servant, without accountability
there will be no application. Without accountability we will
feed on the word with the same kind of selectivity that char-
acterises all young children who pick out the tasty bits on
their plate but fail to eat the less appealing morsels that are
nevertheless 'good for them'! Without accountability,
however well prepared the meal may be, those children who
selectively pick from their plate will end up with an unbal-
anced diet that stunts their growth and leaves them ill-
prepared to face the challenges of adult life. And yet this is
precisely what happens in our churches week upon week,
month upon month, year upon year.

Almost regardless of the denomination we might care to

look at, the most important day of the week for the church
is Sunday, and the most important time for church activity
is the Sunday service. After the worship has been enthusiastically enjoyed by the first three rows, the preaching and
teaching of the word takes place. Finally, after a prayer time
(long or short, standing or lying) the people are dismissed
and the preacher stands by the exit in order to collect the
praise, or otherwise, for all his hard work, as he clings to the
vague hope that something will have taken root and started
to grow in their lives before it gets submerged under the
weight of Sunday lunch.

In most churches the pastor or leader has put a great deal
of time and energy into the preparation of the word for that
meeting, and rightly so as those who preach should do so as
though they were 'speaking the very words of God' (1 Peter
4:11). He may stand up and deliver the word under an
incredible anointing and with an authority that would move
mountains and there may be an altar call where many
respond with genuine displays of emotion. And yet despite
this, when he comes to look at the life of the church the following Sunday morning and attempts to assess the fruit of
all his efforts the previous week, he risks real discourage-
ment. How many lives have been changed? How many of the
people have applied the word to their lives? How many
remember anything of what was said? Apparently, remark-
ably few. Like the sower going into the field the seed of the
word was sown, but the next Sunday, despite his genuine
hope and eager expectation, the fruit just hasn't appeared. In
fact, he has difficulty seeing even a few green shoots poking
out through the dry ground.

The awful truth is this: as preachers and teachers, week
after week we sow much but reap only sparingly. The world
discovered this a long time ago. While only 5–15 per cent of

people apply teaching received in the traditional lecture style, up to 80 per cent will apply knowledge gained through 'mentoring' – which is actually nothing more than a twentieth-century term for discipleship. Secular businesses and organisations have applied themselves to the process of mentoring with enthusiasm and have reaped the benefits accordingly. The church, however, has been commanded by Jesus to implement this 'management style', and yet seems to be incapable of doing the very thing that the world is now showing to be so effective in producing growth. It's time for things to change!

Apathetic agriculture!

Jesus talked to his disciples about the view from his side of the street: he sees an abundantly fruitful harvest field of souls waiting to hear the word of life but very few people to go and harvest it (Luke 10:2). We might say exactly the opposite: we see plenty of people in the church 'field', some even willing to work in it, but very little sign of a fruitful harvest! The seed of the word is sown into the field of our hearts every week but only a small percentage of that seed ever begins to bear fruit in our lives. Now what farmer would be satisfied with that kind of yield? How many farms would still be in existence if they only had a 5 or 10 per cent yield for their sowing? And yet year in, year out we don't seem to learn from our mistakes, preferring to plough the same lonely furrow and 'preaching faithfully' with the ever decreasing expectation that anything or anyone will really change as a result. The word of God may well be living and active in other nations and in other fields, but in our field it seems to be almost lifeless or at the very least semi-comatose, and to make matters worse we don't seem to know what to do about it.

What ground are we sowing into?

Jesus often talked to the crowd in parables. No doubt they found his stories interesting, if rather obscure. On one occasion he spoke to the crowd about a sower who went into the field to sow seed – a nice story using images with which they were all familiar and which seemed to hold the promise of something more by way of interpretation. It was quite obvious that he wasn't telling them a story simply to amuse them, or using it as a commercial break in between the feature presentation of miraculous signs and wonders, nor was he trying to be mystical or 'other-worldly'. But instead of giving them the satisfaction of a detailed explanation, Jesus stopped his preaching prematurely. He did not go on to explain to them what the story was meant to illustrate, or how they were to apply it to their lives.

Frustrated, his disciples came to him later and asked him why he insisted on being so cryptic in his presentation and so unwilling to give a detailed exposition of the word to the crowd who had, after all, come to hear him speak. His answer was blunt:

He replied, 'The knowledge of the secrets of the kingdom of heaven has been given to you, but not to them . . . This is why I speak to them in parables: Though seeing, they do not see; though hearing, they do not hear or understand. In them is fulfilled the prophecy of Isaiah: "You will be ever hearing but never understanding; you will be ever seeing but never perceiving. For this people's heart has become calloused; they hardly hear with their ears, and they have closed their eyes . . ."'
(Matthew 13:11, 13–15)

The truth was, the revelation of the word he spoke was intended only for his own disciples and not for the amusement of the crowd. He chose not to expound the meaning of his parables to the crowd because he knew that they were fundamentally incapable of seeing or hearing the truth due to the condition of their hearts. Hard, calloused hearts are incapable of receiving the word of God and if it cannot be received it cannot be applied. The parable of the sower was intended as a powerful visual aid to illustrate to his disciples the issues that make our own hearts unreceptive to the word. The same is still true today. When we consider the ground the sower sowed the seed into we begin to understand why much of our preaching and teaching bears so little fruit in our own lives as well as the lives of our church members.

The path

Jesus said that the seed that is sown is the word of God (Mark 4:14) and it first falls onto the path. Now a path is unremarkable; it is not a paved road or a major highway; it would not appear on a street map or in a local guidebook. It is merely a well-trodden piece of ground that is found at the edge of the field. It has the same potential for fruitfulness that the rest of the field has, but it cannot reach that potential as long as it continues to remain the path. Something must change before it can produce a good crop.

The path is the familiar route taken by the farmer who comes to sow the seed with seasonal predictability and it represents our church tradition, the well-worn track that we take as we lead our churches through the same liturgy, written or unwritten, week after week. The path is made up of those things that we do because 'we've always done them that way' and that we are unwilling to change because they give us security and comfort and, perhaps most importantly, the ability to control the direction and content of the meeting. The path is symbolic of the denominational inter- pretation and emphasis that we bring to our favourite scrip- tures that have been clearly marked out from the pulpit by years of consistent repetition. We dare not look at them in any other way, even when the Holy Spirit begins to enlighten the eyes of our heart, in case we rock the boat and unsettle the comfortable. The path is the thoroughfare of church organisation, the business and busy-ness of making certain that church 'happens' each week. Tradition, narrow famil- iarity and total predictability all have a deadening effect upon our hearts that makes us unreceptive to the living word whenever it is preached. The soil on the path has become so compacted and the boundaries so rigidly demarcated that it would take a pickaxe wielded by a navvy to turn the soil. And the very prospect of taking a pickaxe to the soil of our traditions threatens our confidence and our security and makes us pace anxiously backward and forward over the ever-hardening ground as we try to justify why we are still doing what we have always done despite the poverty of outcome.

When our hearts become as hard as this it is no wonder that the word doesn't bear fruit in our lives in the way that it should. Dead tradition makes for a bad harvest – it is the devil's bird table (Matthew 13:4), keeping him alive and healthy as the church continues through its icy cold winter season. No wonder many of our churches are so small in number and insignificant in their impact on society. We need the pickaxe of the Holy Spirit to break our traditions and break our hearts. We need the brokenness that only God can bring to turn over the hard ground that is to be found there.

The rocky ground

So many of us live our Christian lives like the main character in the story of Dr Jekyll and Mr Hyde. We lead a 'second life' – a life very different to the one that is brought to church each Sunday and which is well hidden from those we sit next to each week. Somehow, as we step out of the car in the church car park, a transformation takes place and we clothe ourselves with our well-rehearsed insincerity just in time to take up our regular seat inside the church. With luck no one apart from our immediate family will see the transformation that takes place as our 'second life' gives way for a few short hours each week to our respectable, acceptable 'first life' – the life that we are known and loved for at church.

But our 'second life' is the life of compromise, the reflection of our character, or lack of it. We have already been through the Bible and have cut out the verses we like the best, those that don't offend our sensibilities or oblige us to change our ways, and have pasted them into our own book, *The Gospel According to Our Armchair*. Superficially, things look fine, but just under the surface there is a shallowness that makes fruitfulness impossible. No amount of preaching into that kind of heart will produce a good harvest. As the word is preached we might make a genuine response at an altar call as the good seed falls into the rocky ground. We might experience a repentant spirit that accompanies a genuine acknowledgement of sin, but the rocky ground is unable to produce fruit in keeping with that 'repentance' because the roots cannot penetrate the hardness of the underlying rock. As soon as the sincerity of that repentance is tested the roots give way, the plant is torn out and the harvest is lost.

As preachers or pastors, how many times have we seen the same faces coming to the front of the church, weeping tears of 'repentance' and declaring that they have turned their back on their sin, only to find them there again the next week, and the next, and the next, confessing the same sins and praying the same prayers for God to show them mercy? Their second life always seems to take the upper hand and thwarts the work of grace that God, as well as the pastor, is looking for in their heart week after week. Unless our second life is put to death, crucified along with all our fleshly desires and passions that feed it and keep it alive, we will only have shallow soil in which the word can begin to grow. In soil like this there can be no fruitful harvest. Again, only the pickaxe of the Holy Spirit can expose the hidden, underlying rock in our hearts and bring the brokenness that he requires for true fruitfulness.

The thorny ground

Competition has no place in the kingdom of God. Wherever there is a spirit of competition in the church there is also a limit to our fruitfulness and the size of the harvest we can reap. Competition 'caps' our growth and blights our precious crop. This principle was clearly laid down in the Old Testament when God gave his laws to his people through Moses, and yet we may easily overlook it because the context in which it is found does not seem to be immediately relevant in our technological age. God said: 'Do not plant two kinds of seed in your vineyard; if you do, not only the crops you plant but also the fruit of the vineyard will be defiled' (Deuteronomy 22:9).

When two seeds of different types are planted in the same field, competition for the available ground begins immediately. This is not the fault of the seed; it is the nature of the seed. The seed that germinates most rapidly and takes root most efficiently will win the race to possess the ground, but only at the expense of the fruitfulness of the other seed that was sown. The Holy Spirit used this natural example of competition to illustrate the spiritual principle he wanted his people to grasp: competition brings defilement to the harvest. Whenever there is competition for the ground of our heart, where the things of the world compete for our affection and attention and take our eyes away from God, a defilement enters into the vineyard that effects a reduction in our fruitfulness.

The thorny ground represents the heart that has placed its confidence in anything other than God; the heart that prefers to listen to the whispers or the shouts of the devil promising security outside of God's provision through what we can have and own. The thorny ground represents the heart cluttered by the cares of twenty-first-century life and the pursuit of selfish pleasure (Luke 8:14) over the pursuit of intimacy with Jesus. How many of us, when honestly examining our hearts, can say that we have escaped the influence of these kinds of deep-rooted weeds? How many times have we had to deal with them, tearing them from the ground of our hearts and throwing them onto the fire, only to discover that a few weeks or months later they have reappeared as strong and as healthy as ever because our previous efforts have failed to deal effectively with the root?

The farmer strikes back

We have become so used to the nice 'gospel presentation' of the parable of the sower, even to the point where we use it as justification for our own lack of success in evangelism ('Oh dear, they didn't receive what I had to say – it just fell on rocky ground'), that we are in danger of missing the serious implications for our own hearts. The writer to the Hebrews helps to make things more clear:

> Land that drinks in the rain often falling on it and that produces a crop useful to those for whom it is farmed receives the blessing of God. But land that produces thorns and thistles is worthless and is in danger of being cursed. In the end it will be burned. (Hebrews 6:7–8)

If our hearts continue to produce only thorns and thistles instead of a crop useful for those for whom it is farmed, we are in danger of living under a curse rather than the blessing of God. Thorny ground is not only unproductive; in God's eyes it is worthless. In the end it will be burned. Jesus talked about the unproductive branch of the vine in John 15, saying that if we do not remain in him we will wither and die and that 'such branches are picked up, thrown into the fire and burned'. Now theologians may argue about what that means. Does it mean we lose our salvation or does it mean we lose our reward? Does it mean we just don't produce a very good harvest or does it mean something completely different? I am not willing to speculate about the interpretation of that passage but one thing I am certain about: whatever it means, it doesn't sound good! I want to do everything within my power to avoid that kind of burning! And in fact, all we need to do in order to avoid it is to get rid of the thorns of competition and strife that defile our harvest. Jeremiah tells us what we must do:

> This is what the LORD says to the men of Judah and to Jerusalem: 'Break up your unploughed ground and do not sow among thorns. Circumcise yourselves to the LORD, circumcise

your hearts, you men of Judah and people of Jerusalem, or my wrath will break out and burn like fire because of the evil you have done – burn with no-one to quench it. (Jeremiah 4:3–4)

The sins of the thorny ground (for that is what they are) can only be dealt with by using the 'holy rotavator'. Thorny ground cannot be 'tidied up'; it must be broken up. It cannot be left fallow and at the same time be expected to produce a good harvest of fruit. Sowing the word among thorns is a waste of good seed, and for that reason God says, 'Don't do it!' Only hearts that have been adequately broken by the Holy Spirit can bear the kind of harvest God is looking for.

Cutting down or cutting off?

The solution to the unfruitfulness of the 'thorny ground' is as surprising as it is painful: circumcision. Jeremiah tells us that God wants the ground to be broken up and, changing the metaphor, our hearts to be circumcised. The covenant of circumcision was first established between God and his people as a sign to them of the unique relationship that they were to have with him. It was a continual reminder to them of their responsibility to serve God as a holy nation, his treasured possession amid the depravity of a pagan world. And this symbolism of separation to God, if not the practice of physical circumcision, was carried over into the Christian world. In the same way that physical circumcision indicated separation from the world, so the circumcision of the heart performed by Jesus would indicate our separation from sin and its attractions. But Jeremiah says that we have a part to play in this ongoing circumcision process: 'Circumcise *yourselves* to the Lord' (Jeremiah 4:4, my italics) he tells us. How are we to do this? What does that mean? I may want the ground of my heart to be able to receive the word of God and to produce a fruitful harvest, but how am I to perform this task of circumcision?

Becoming a follower

One thing is clear from Scripture: with the possible exception of Abraham there are no recorded examples of anyone performing circumcision on themselves! For obvious reasons it always takes the steady hand of someone else who can be trusted implicitly to perform this service! Only in the context of a trusting relationship can the heart be safely circumcised; a relationship where the one whose heart is being circumcised knows that the one who is performing it has already walked that path of pain, vulnerability and brokenness himself. Discipleship, as Jesus intends it to be, is far more than simply being held to account for the way in which we conduct ourselves or apply the word that has been preached from the pulpit on Sunday. It is a willingness to follow someone who has the lifestyle and character of the Lord Jesus; someone who has already submitted themselves to the Holy Spirit's painful work of ploughing the ground of their own heart, and who is demonstrating the fruitful harvest of righteousness that such submission brings. Such a person will not demand submission or extract obedience from the one they are influencing for good and for God; they will simply set the example of a Christ-like lifestyle and invite the other person to join them as together they grow more like Jesus in thought, word and deed. Only in this kind of setting will there be the necessary trust and security for traditional values to be safely challenged, shallowness of character confronted, misplaced affections redirected and more thorny ground ploughed.

Change is here to stay

I knew that the effectiveness of my preaching and the preaching of others was being contained by the lack of this kind of relationship within the church. As a result the harvest of righteousness in our own lives and the harvest of souls in our region was suffering from a blight that threatened the continued growth of the kingdom of God. The challenge for us as a church, and in particular for Lois and myself as the leaders of the church, was how we were to displace the centre of gravity in the life of the church. The gravitational pull of Sunday 'activities' and a 'Sunday = church' mentality, where the opportunity for becoming a follower is highly limited, needed to be transformed into a lifestyle of discipleship, where the truth of the word that lived and bore fruit in our own lives became a challenge for others to follow our example. Paul was able to say to the Corinthian church: 'Follow my example, as I follow the example of Christ' (1 Corinthians 11:1). We began to appreciate that traditional church structures often militated against this process, and so began the transition from our traditional church structure into cell church.

What do you do with it?

When the Holy Spirit turned up in our church in 1994 we became the host to people from churches throughout the region and then the world who wanted to see what God was doing. We did not want to keep it to, or for, ourselves, and after 18 months, people had come to the church, received from God and taken the blessing home to their own church where he continued to work in the same way.

But as we visited these congregations over the coming

years we discovered a worrying trend that threatened to prevent the work that the Holy Spirit was wanting to do throughout the whole church. We noticed that there was a tendency to 'attach' what God was doing to an existing structure rather than to demolish the structures, sometimes built in error, and rebuild with new plans. Many churches seemed to have embarked on a programme of home improvements that accommodated and made room for the new thing rather than completely remodelling from the foundations up. We quickly realised that if we were to be obedient to the Holy Spirit we should not back off from the issues of discipleship through fear of losing control, or fear of too much control, or from bad past experience of discipleship movements. Jesus called us to be disciples and to make disciples and that was his blueprint for building the church. If we weren't doing it then we weren't building the church in the way he wanted it to be built. But before we could introduce another change into the life of the church we needed to be clear of the implications and cost that such a change would incur.

Jesus said:

'Suppose one of you wants to build a tower. Will he not first sit down and estimate the cost to see if he has enough money to complete it? For if he lays the foundation and is not able to finish it, everyone who sees it will ridicule him, saying, "This fellow began to build and was not able to finish."' (Luke 14:28–30)

We did not want to be guilty of enthusiastically laying the foundation only to discover that we did not have the wherewithal to complete it. And so we began to look at Jesus' experience with his disciples to see how he responded to the challenges that we would undoubtedly face as we in turn started to look for people who would follow us wherever the Lord took us.

LIFE APPLICATION

Think back to last Sunday. What were the main points in the sermon? What passage of Scripture was used? Who was the preacher? What has the word of God that was preached one week ago changed or produced in your life, or in the life of your family?

Who, if anyone, do you have a discipleship relationship with? Who is discipling you through godly example and influence? Who are you discipling?

PRAYER

Father I want your word to bear fruit in my life and in the lives of others. Please lead me to the person or people you have chosen who will hold me to account as a disciple. Help me to honour them as we work together to be true disciples of Jesus. Amen.

9

No More Excuses

Then Jesus came to them and said, '. . . go and make disciples . . .'

Matthew 28:18–19

Have you ever stopped to ask yourself *why* you make some of the decisions that you make in life? What makes you decide to select one item in preference to another, or influences you to do one thing rather than another? When the time comes to buy a new car, for example, what factors influence your choice of one model over another? And what is the most significant factor that influences you when you decide to buy a new shirt, or a new pair of shoes, or one brand of biscuits over another brand on the supermarket shelf? You might think the answer is incredibly obvious: the decision as to whether or not you buy something is most strongly influenced by what you can afford to pay. But is that actually the main determinant? In reality, probably not.

In Britain, when legislation relating to the regulation of the credit industry was relaxed, an explosion of lending took place that quickly resulted in the nation being plunged into debt. Such was the desire of people to 'have' things that it wasn't long before we had spent far more than we could actually afford, with a cumulative personal debt equivalent to

£1,000 for every man, woman and child in the country. Clearly, not being able to afford something didn't seem to be much of a disincentive to 'owning' it! Whether we could afford something or not had ceased to become the strongest factor influencing choice and instead the strongest influence became how the ownership of that 'thing' would make us feel. The new car would make us look and feel more important, so we must have it. The new furniture would make us feel more confident when we invited guests to our home, so we couldn't do without it. The new computer would make us feel that we were on the cutting edge of technology and the premium brand biscuits would make us feel confident that we really were caring for our children's wellbeing in the best possible way.

We need only look at the kind of advertising campaigns that we are exposed to in order to see that they are specifically designed to make us feel that we are missing out on something if we don't own it, and reassure us that we will feel so much better if we do! How we feel now or how we *will* feel has become the single most important factor determining choice in our society. Feeling 'bad' or 'uncomfortable' about ourselves is not an option that we are even prepared to contemplate – in fact we are positively discouraged from tolerating any feeling of discomfort whatsoever. A multimillion pound service industry has grown up around the need to make us feel entirely comfortable in every way possible and at all times, and in an increasingly 'consumer-led' society we are encouraged to complain loudly if we don't get exactly what we want, exactly when we want it.

Are you sitting comfortably?

Now there is nothing wrong in itself with feeling good or being comfortable, but when this becomes our predominant motivation in life, invading every area of our being and influencing our every decision, we run the risk of becoming overwhelmingly selfish in our outlook. Relationships that cease to satisfy our immediate needs or fail to live up to our personal expectations can be justifiably terminated regardless of the impact on the other person or persons involved. Babies that are conceived 'by accident' and become an inconvenience can be disposed of legitimately for no other reason than that they would interfere with our acquisitive lifestyle. Even food that has failed to come up to our expectation, not because it is nutritionally deficient but simply because it is visually unappealing, can be discarded without thought, while we sit and watch millions die from starvation on our television screens each day. (Although we might be tempted to turn the television off because those images make us feel too uncomfortable and spoil our appetite!)

It seems clear that the Western world has developed a fixation with the need for personal comfort and ease that has been elevated to a position of priority and importance far above that of the law of God. As a result, most of the decisions we make throughout life have as their primary motivation the need to satisfy our personal craving for self-fulfilment and pleasure, which is of course one of the main hallmarks of sin. Sadly, we see this characteristic demonstrated by many Christians who use the same criteria of consumerism to determine what is 'right' for them in all areas of their life. And nowhere does this become more obvious than when the time comes for them to select the church that they will condescend to join. The first question that Western Christians will often ask when considering a new church, either consciously or subconsciously, is this: 'How will *this* church best meet *my* needs?' This question is then closely followed by a series of supplementary questions that probe even deeper into the way in which this church may make us feel good about ourselves:

'Does this church have good Bible teaching?'

This can be translated as meaning: 'Does the preacher agree with my doctrine and say the sort of things that I want to hear and with which I am comfortably familiar?' There is an implied reward for the co-operative preacher who does not offend his potential new member: 'If he doesn't make me feel uncomfortable or unsettle my lifestyle in any way then this must be the right place for me – and I'll join!'

'What is the pastoral care like in this church?'

This is only another way of saying: 'Am *I* going to get looked after properly and have *my* needs comprehensively met? If I am considered to be the hub around which everything else in the church rotates then this *must* be the right church for me, because I will certainly feel good about myself.'

'Does the style of worship music used here suit my own personal musical tastes and does the physical appearance of the church appeal to me?'

This sounds innocent enough but often hides a more self-centred motive: 'Will I find the corporate meetings an embarrassment to endure or an experience that entertains, and will these pews actually be comfortable enough for the twenty-first-century bottom?'

'Will there be an opportunity for me to use my gifting in this church?'

Brother Humble is actually thinking to himself: 'After all, I have so much to offer these people and God wouldn't have given all of these gifts to me if there wasn't going to be an opening for me to use them in the church.' Unfortunately the underlying motive recognised by everyone but the person who wants to 'serve' the church in this way is this: 'I have a deep-seated need for recognition in order to build up my insecure self-image. I must be able to find an opportunity to establish a power-base for myself from which I can begin to influence people, gain a measure of control over them and "help" them come to understand what a favoured and anointed man of God I am.' People who think like this have forgotten that God's word says that the gift itself makes way for them and does not require self-promotion in order for it to be recognised (Proverbs 18:16).

Now these caricatures are just that – caricatures. But anyone who has been in church leadership for even a short length of time will be only too familiar with these dear people. The question on the bottom line that they need to have answered before they can select the church they are going to join is more often a matter of 'Will I *feel comfortable* here?' than the more important question that the Holy Spirit is wanting to hear, 'Am I being called to *serve others* here?' Unwittingly they are using the personal 'need-centred' values of the crowd rather than the self-sacrificial values of the true disciples of Jesus to help them make their decision. People like this will often join a church for a short while but somehow don't ever seem to bring themselves to the point where they can throw in their lot with the pastor's vision, and often leave muttering spiritual clichés that are really no more than excuses – excuses that demonstrate their unwillingness to feel even slightly uncomfortable in their new church.

Some of these clichés will sound all too familiar to you. For instance, they may say something like, 'I left because I just wasn't being fed . . .' (that is, with the sort of things they wanted to hear!). No one could deny that Jesus was a great Bible teacher. Even as a young child he amazed those who heard him by the depth and the maturity of the answers he gave to their questions that came from his understanding of God's word (Luke 2:47). He may not have been to any rabbinical schools or passed any formal exams in Hebrew theology, but his comprehension of the word of God was second to none and his exposition of Scripture was powerful and consistent with his lifestyle. Even the crowds were impressed by his teaching abilities:

> When Jesus had finished saying these things, the crowds were amazed at his teaching, because he taught as one who had authority, and not as their teachers of the law. (Matthew 7:28–29)

There was no doubt about it; Jesus was a great teacher. He taught the Bible well and the crowd had every opportunity to be 'well fed', as did his disciples. But is 'good Bible teaching' or 'being well fed' the same as 'feeling comfortable'? I don't think his disciples or the members of the crowd felt comfortable at some of the things he had to say to them. He certainly didn't consult them first about their personal doctrinal position before he began to teach them about something he had received from his Father, or ask them which subject they would most like to have him speak on next time he had the opportunity. And he certainly didn't seem to mind if what he had to say upset or offended them. In fact at times it seemed as though he was going out of his way to upset them.

> Jesus said to them, 'I tell you the truth, unless you can eat the flesh of the Son of Man and drink his blood, you have no life in you. Whoever eats my flesh and drinks my blood has eternal life,

and I will raise him up at the last day. For my flesh is real food and my blood is real drink. Whoever eats my flesh and drinks my blood remains in me, and I in him. Just as the living Father sent me and I live because of the Father, so the one who feeds on me will live because of me.' (John 6:53–57)

Now let's be honest – that wasn't exactly a crowd-pleasing sermon, was it? Nor was it immediately obvious what he actually meant by 'eat my flesh and drink my blood'! It wasn't presented with the help of an eye-catching illustration or a visual aid to help them understand its 'deeper meaning' and apply it to their lives. He just threw it out there, into the crowd, and walked off leaving them to deal with it. They simply had to decide whether or not they were going to continue to follow him. The reaction of many of his disciples was similar to the reaction of many visitors and so-called members of our churches today. They found this teaching offensive and hard to accept:

> On hearing it, many of his disciples said, 'This is a hard teaching. Who can accept it?' Aware that his disciples were grumbling about this, Jesus said to them, 'Does this offend you?' (John 6:60–61)

The Holy Spirit often offends our mind in order to reveal our heart, presenting us with food that is hard to swallow but testing the depth and intimacy of our relationship with him and our willingness, or otherwise, to press on and follow him by our response. When our minds are offended in this way we often find that our heart's response is less than wholesome! It is at this point that we must make the choice: either we follow Jesus and allow him to deal with the issues of our hearts on the way, or we fall behind and are left to ruminate on the offence and lick our wounds. Some of Jesus' disciples joined in with the crowd and began to grumble among themselves about this difficult and offensive teaching and before too long many of them had decided it was time to leave: 'From this time many of his disciples turned back and no longer followed him' (John 6:66).

On that day a significant number of his congregation decided it was time to look elsewhere, and many more decided not to join 'his church' on the basis of that one sermon alone – his preaching was just too uncomfortable and too unsettling for their delicate stomachs. They were being well fed, but they were being fed strong meat and some of them found themselves with a bad case of heartburn. No doubt they left him muttering to themselves, 'We're leaving! We just wouldn't get properly fed here! Look at what he wants to give us to eat! He wants us to eat his flesh and drink his blood! How healthy is that?'

'I wasn't being properly fed' is often nothing more than an excuse used by the person who is leaving in an attempt to pass the blame for their inability to accept the truth that is being presented to them back onto the shoulders of the preacher or the leader of the church, while absolving them from any responsibility whatsoever in working through the issues. When this happens, as all too often it does, how does this make us feel as church leaders? Does it spur us into frenzied action as we chase after the departing 'member', trying to persuade him or her to return to the fold? Does it pour cold water on the Spirit's fire, sending us into a downward spiral of self-despair, or does it make us back-pedal and apologise in the hope of retaining their favour?

Consumer-led or Holy-Spirit-led?

Look at what Jesus did when he saw them leaving in droves, or rather look at what he didn't do. Jesus didn't chase after those people who were offended by what he had had to say. He didn't write a 'positional paper' to clarify his views and he didn't offer them counselling sessions or pastoral appointments so they could discuss their concerns regarding his teaching. He wasn't trying to please the crowd – he was treating them as his disciples. Jesus presented his disciples with the word he had received from his Father (John 12:50) and having delivered it, he left them to make up their mind as to what they would do with it. Would they follow him or would they leave? There was no attempt at persuasion, no heavy enforcement, no emotional blackmail, no subtle coercion. He just shared the word from the Father, put it into practice in his own life and, looking over his shoulder at them, was heard to say, 'Are you coming with me?' On this occasion, evidently many of them weren't.

Another excuse you may hear is, 'I left because there was no pastoral care . . .' Did Jesus' disciples receive pastoral care and input from Jesus? Of course they did. But would many Christians nowadays recognise the kind of pastoral care that Jesus gave his disciples as being either adequate or appropriate for their own needs? Almost certainly not! How many church leaders nowadays would dare to say to their people: 'Foxes have holes and birds of the air have nests, but if you follow me I can't guarantee you'll have a bed to go to at the end of each day' (Luke 9:57 – my paraphrase)? How many would say, 'Don't bother going back to bury your dead father – let the dead bury themselves. Just follow me!' (Luke 9:59–60 – paraphrased) or 'If you decide to follow my example don't forget to bring your own cross – you're going to need it!' (Mark 8:34 – paraphrased)?

We have somehow translated 'pastoral care' into a very consumer sensitive, people-pleasing concept, not at all like Jesus viewed it in relation to his followers. He loved his disciples deeply and provided for their needs at a practical level but his heart was to equip them for active service, not to promote self-indulgent navel gazing. If we began to preach these same uncompromising principles of discipleship in our churches today we might find that there was a sudden and significant drop in attendance the following Sunday morning. But why shouldn't we preach the same things? And if people did leave as a result of our preaching what would that say about them as disciples of Jesus anyway? After all, the entry criteria for following Jesus in the twenty-first-century are no different today than they were in Jesus' day. But even if we do have the courage to preach these principles and put them into practice in our own lives first, the church has developed a set of stock answers that we fall back on to avoid facing up to the real issues they present us with. Our response to such challenges as these has been neatly spiritualised by years of clever exegesis and traditional interpretation, so that through a kind of intellectual word play the implications and cost of true discipleship can be avoided:

- 'No guarantee of a bed at the end of the day,' we read. And of course we agree with it in principle, but prefer to apply it to Christians in the Third World or at least somewhere outside of our own country. But when the reality of discipleship starts to bite in this way and our earthly 'securities' are threatened, our attitude changes. We say, 'We must be doing something wrong! We are clearly being demonically oppressed! This is spiritual warfare! We bind you, foul spirit of poverty, in the name of Jesus!'
- 'Your father has just died – I'm so sorry to hear that,' we say empathetically. 'Well, we offer you our sincere condolences and welcome you to our post-bereavement counsel-

ling class this Thursday led by our trained counselling staff. In time, when you have recovered perhaps you might like to consider joining one of our monthly men's groups where you can have fellowship with other men who have gone through the same painful life event. You probably won't have much time for anything else (like discipleship) but at least you'll be on the road to being completely healed.'

- 'Take up your cross,' we read rather uncertainly. 'This is obviously a wonderful allegory, although we're not quite sure what he is actually referring to, but we think that it is probably the sickness that is afflicting you, or your difficult family circumstances! Surely they must be the only cross you would have to bear! But *we* won't ask you to do anything that might make you feel at all uncomfortable. In this church we have the motto: "Your needs come first" and we intend to continue that way.'

Pastoral care *is* important. One of the Ephesians 4 ministry gifts is that of pastor or pastor/teacher (Ephesians 4:11–13). But this office is given to the church to prepare God's people for works of *service,* so that we become more like Jesus in every respect and so that the body of Christ may be built up. They are not given to cushion us into years of inactivity and slothfulness while the rest of the world goes to hell.

A third excuse might be, 'I left because they didn't recognise my gift . . . (Can't they see how much God favours me?)' Among the most frustrating people who come to join the church are those who firmly believe they are God's particular gift to whatever deficiency they perceive to be present in your current structure. They are the evangelist 'you have been waiting for all your life'. They are the children's pastor that will soon have your children's work licked into shape.

They are the prophet who will give you wise counsel direct from the throne of God so that you no longer need to worry about leadership decisions in the future. They are the inter-cessor/youth pastor/worship leader/solo singer – in fact they are anyone who they perceive will get a prominent position in the life of the church and that commands respect from those less gifted than themselves. It is strange how few people come boldly offering their services for the toilet cleaning rota because this is their 'gift from God'. And yet Jesus said about himself: 'For even the Son of Man did not come to be served, but to serve' (Mark 10:45).

Jesus understood that he had come with the express purpose of being obedient to the commands of his Father and that that would not be a path of comfort but of discom-fort, a path of pain, self-sacrifice and death, not of revelling in the adulation of the crowd. And Jesus made it plain that he expected no less from his own disciples. If they had their heart set on position he was only too ready to burst their bubble and inject some reality into their lives!

Who am I?

One day Jesus asked his disciples who the people thought he was. They replied, 'Some say John the Baptist; others say Elijah; and still others, that one of the prophets of long ago has come back to life' (Luke 9:19). There was obviously some debate among the crowd as to his true identity, but it was clear that whoever he was, he was someone important and famous. His presence among them usually resulted in something miraculous taking place, and therefore he was a good person to have around. I suspect that his disciples also enjoyed the influence and power that their close relationship with Jesus brought them. The crowd would obviously see that his disciples were the 'specially chosen' confidants of this important celebrity and whether they thought like the disciples that he was their long-awaited Messiah or merely a resurrected national hero, it was good for their own egos to be around him.

Jesus was quick to identify this and to bring the necessary correction to their way of thinking. 'But what about you?' he asked. 'Who do you say I am?' Peter answered, 'The Christ of God' (Luke 9:20). Peter made this bold declaration of his faith, nailing his colours firmly to the mast. He was absolutely correct, having received this revelation direct from the heart of the Father himself (Matthew 16:17). But what else lay just beneath the surface of Peter's heart when he said this? Perhaps he was thinking, 'You are the One we've all been waiting to meet for so long – and now you're here with us. You are the One who will deliver us from our enemies and restore Israel to its rightful place – and we're your friends! Our fathers may have dreamed of this day, but we are not only seeing it, we're spending all day, every day, with the Messiah. Now how important does that make us?' No doubt the people in the crowd would have asked, 'Why them, and not me? What do they have that I don't? What makes them so special?' Jesus must have been well aware of the danger of this kind of prideful thinking and so he was straight onto their case:

And he said, 'The Son of Man must suffer many things and be rejected by the elders, chief priests and teachers of the law, and he must be killed and on the third day be raised to life.' Then he said to them all: 'If anyone would come after me, he must deny himself and take up his cross daily and follow me. For whoever wants to save his life will lose it, but whoever loses his life for me will save it.' (Luke 9:22–24)

Essentially Jesus was reminding them that at the heart of discipleship is not the adoration or popular acclaim of the crowd but rather a lifestyle of brokenness and death. Far from being the conquering military king that traditional expectation placed upon Jesus as the Messiah, he was to be the suffering servant who would experience complete rejection by the crowd and be put to death by religious zealots. More uncomfortably, Jesus was making it quite clear that anyone who wanted to be one of his disciples would have to be willing to experience the same sacrificial lifestyle and death to personal goals and ambition. Jesus was not looking for 'gifted' men and women to be his disciples, those with personality or natural skills that could be used to promote his cause. He was looking for those who would obey his word and follow him wherever he led them – even if it meant they followed him to their death. And Jesus is still looking for those qualities in our lives and the lives of our churches and his disciples today. Those who come offering their 'gifts' in exchange for position should remember the example of their Saviour. Jesus' 'gifts' resulted in his torture, crucifixion and death. Why should we think our lesser gifts deserve anything better?

Once bitten, twice shy

Just like every other leader in the church, we had heard those same excuses repeated by prospective church members time and time again as they slammed the door on the way out. Down through the years we had watched people come and go, arriving with great fanfare and leaving at the first sign of personal discomfort or simply after all their attempts to gain a platform and personal recognition had failed. It was not so much that they were unwilling to be taught, but that they were unwilling to follow anyone other than themselves. Unless they achieved the position or recognition that they thought they deserved they would never be willing to follow anyone, and even then they would only have followed for as long as they retained their position.

As we began to build the church once again we realised that we must use the same principles that Jesus had used – that of teaching his disciples by example and not cajoling the crowd into a reluctant acceptance of the vision that God was entrusting to us by the promise of position or reward. But as we considered the way forward and the steps that the Holy Spirit was clearly calling us to take, we began to appreciate the masterstroke that the devil had delivered against the church by perverting our understanding of the principles of discipleship and dragging the very word itself through the mire of disrepute. It seemed as though every use of the word 'discipleship' in church leadership circles was linked to a negative connotation or experience because someone had either personally experienced difficulties or knew of someone who had been traumatised through the excesses of the discipleship movement.

The truth is that discipleship has received a good deal of bad press in the last few decades and in some cases with clear justification. In some situations it became little more than a thinly veiled disguise for control and domination that produced enormous hurt and great injury to many earnest Christians. The backlash provoked by this kind of extreme abuse has made the church at large understandably very cautious about anything that appears to be resurrecting values that even suggest these earlier excesses. But discipleship is not wrong in itself. After all, Jesus didn't suggest we make disciples – he commanded it! Wrong discipleship, however, is always wrong in the same way as a bad apple is always bad. But no one would suggest we should stop eating apples just because we had bitten into a bad one in the past. David Watson, a noted British church leader of the 1970s, once said, 'The right response to abuse is not disuse but proper use.' We must be careful to apply this to the process of building the church so that we overcome the damage that the devil has sought to inflict upon us in attempting to discredit discipleship.

What's the difference?

So what distinguishes abusive 'discipleship' from godly discipleship? The answer to this question could be the subject of a book in itself, but has already been alluded to earlier in this chapter when we considered Jesus' handling of his own disciples. There are three key principles that will help us from falling into the errors of the past:

1. The person who is discipling must be intimate with Jesus

It is out of that intimacy that God's wisdom is revealed and God's way is delineated. It is out of that intimacy that humility is birthed and true authority imparted. Without the characteristics of brokenness and sacrifice that come from this intimacy there can be no true discipleship. Paul said: 'I want to know Christ and the power of his resurrection and the fellowship of sharing in his sufferings' (Philippians 3:10).

Paul wanted to know Jesus intimately, to know his resurrection power in the same way *and* to share in the fellowship of his sufferings. Because his life clearly demonstrated these characteristics he was bold enough to say: 'Follow my example, as I follow the example of Christ' (1 Corinthians

11:1). He was expecting his own disciples to follow him only inasmuch as he followed Christ's example; an example that was one of self-sacrifice, humility, brokenness and the fear of God that flowed out of intimacy with his Father. Intimacy with the Father was the foundation of Jesus' life and the means of his own successful discipling (Luke 6:12–13). If we are to have followers we must first make absolutely certain that we are closely following Jesus' example of self-sacrifice.

2. The discipler must make being a disciple his or her priority and the process of making disciples secondary

All true discipleship relationships demonstrate this important characteristic. Obeying God personally is more important than obliging other people to obey God. At the start of the twenty-first century people are less interested in simply being told what the answer is; they want to see it in action – seeing *is* believing! At the beginning of the first century Jesus had already made that the foundation of his church growth policy.

> Therefore *go and make disciples of all nations*, baptising them in the name of the Father and of the Son and of the Holy Spirit, and *teaching them to obey everything I have commanded you*. (Matthew 28:19–20, my italics)

It is only as we obey the commands of Jesus ourselves that we have not only the right but also the ability to ask other people to follow us. In the same way that only sheep can produce sheep and only cows can produce more cows, so too only disciples can produce disciples. If we aren't demonstrating obedience to Jesus' commands in our own lives we have no right to expect it from those who are following us.

3. Godly discipling does not impose authority but always gives the person who is following the freedom to choose

After Jesus had preached his tough 'flesh and blood' sermon and his disciples began to leave he could easily have become discouraged. But despite the reaction of his own disciples he personally demonstrated the most important attribute of being a true disciple – he feared God more than he feared man. It did not matter that his influence might decline or that his ministry would not prosper and succeed – he feared God and that was more important than anything else. At the moment where personal securities are tested he was able to turn to his closest disciples and say: 'You do not want to leave too, do you?' (John 6:67).

Jesus was not trying to impose his will on his disciples, even though he was the most accomplished discipler this world has ever known. He knew what the Father had revealed to him and that was all that really mattered – he just wanted to know if his closest followers were still willing to come after him. True discipling does not depend on charisma, personal gifting or people management skills; it depends on hearing God and following him regardless of who or how many follow.

As we honestly examined the style of church and church leadership that we had become familiar with we realised that, like so many other church leaders, we had settled for something a long way short of God's ideal, and therefore God's best for us. There were some major changes in our understanding that were going to have to take place, and some even larger changes in our working practice. But we knew that if we were going to make the disciples that Jesus expected rather than the converts that we had won (and lost) in the past then these changes had to be implemented immediately.

LIFE APPLICATION

Think of the church you currently attend. What motivated you to join that church?

What was the last 'difficult' sermon you heard preached? What was your response? Who helped hold you to account? What was the outcome in your life?

Have you ever felt frustrated that your 'gift' was not recognised? What did you do about it? Did you try and promote yourself or crucify your ambition?

PRAYER

Dear Father, I am so thankful that your Son Jesus was willing to give up everything for my sake. Thank you, Jesus, for your humble obedience that took you to the cross and made you willing to despise its shame for the joy of having me as one of your disciples. I ask you now, Holy Spirit, to help me to put to death every selfish desire and make me willing to be an obedient disciple of Jesus in every way. Amen.

10

Core Values

All a man's ways seem innocent to him, but motives are weighed by the LORD.

Proverbs 16:2

One of the more fashionable management concepts of recent years that has found its way into many diverse areas of life, including that of the church, is the need for an organisation to have a Mission Statement. Mission Statements define the purpose of the organisation in a way that helps all those involved to better appreciate the goal that they are collectively working towards. If you are a company that manufactures elastic bands, your Mission Statement might run something like this:

We aim to make the highest quality elastic bands possible, employing the most cost-efficient methods and using only locally grown rubber.

With a Mission Statement like that you know exactly what you are supposed to be making, those things that are considered important factors in the manufacturing process and precisely where you are going to look for the raw materials you require. Now if the managing director of this company decided to come down on to the shop floor one day, and instead of discovering that his company was manufacturing 'the highest quality elastic bands possible, employing the most cost-efficient methods and using only locally grown rubber' he discovered that they were actually making low quality paper clips from imported foreign steel, he would be faced with a significant challenge and the need to make an immediate decision. Either the company would have to revise their Mission Statement and bring it in line with what they were actually producing, or alternatively they would have to stop what they were doing and start to bring their productivity in line with their Mission Statement. In this sort of situation a Mission Statement can be a useful tool, enabling an organisation to examine how effectively it is achieving the aims and objectives that it has set for itself.

What is the right decision to make?

Mission Statements can also enable those responsible for leading the organisation to assess each decision that is made in the light of the agreed purpose that has been laid down in its statement. 'Will this decision help to further the aims and objectives of the organisation or not?' 'If we decide to do this or that how will that help us achieve our goal?' Mission Statements can be used continually to assess whether an organisation is doing what it is supposed to be doing or if it has lost the plot altogether. At first sight they certainly seem to be good news, and they can be very helpful in establishing the effectiveness, or otherwise, of an organisation in the market-place. But they can bring with them their fair share of problems too!

A friend of mine told me of how his company management

had decided that they needed to have a Mission Statement (after all, everyone else had got one and they didn't want to be left out!). And so they gave their highly paid senior management an entire afternoon to brainstorm, in the hope that the distillation of their collective thoughts and ideas would produce a wonderful Mission Statement by the end of the day that they could proudly display to whoever wanted to see it! After many hours of discussion they came up with a phrase that they felt encapsulated the thrust of their organisation and promptly set about getting it printed on high quality paper, putting an impressive frame around it and hanging it on the wall. A few months down the line they made an alarming discovery. Despite the hours of deliberation, despite the quality of the paper it had been printed on and the impressive nature of the frame that surrounded it, the Mission Statement had made no significant impact whatsoever on the running of the organisation. In fact, the only positive thing that it had done was to cover up a patch on a corridor wall that had previously been in need of decoration. The problem was this: people walked past it every day, but no one ever read it, much less applied it to their lives in such a way that their behaviour or attitudes were influenced or changed by it. Whatever its merits as a piece of written English or clever management-speak, to most people working there it was entirely irrelevant.

The most important Mission Statement ever written

Jesus was responsible for formulating the most important Mission Statement ever written. In it he outlined the aims and objectives of his 'organisation', his expectations for each one of his workers and the means by which he planned for growth. He said:

Therefore go and make disciples of all nations, baptising them
in the name of the Father and of the Son and of the Holy Spirit,
and teaching them to obey everything I have commanded you.
(Matthew 28:19–20)

These were the last instructions that Jesus left with the
church before ascending to heaven, and of course we are all
very familiar with these verses which we have called the
'Great Commission'. As far as I can see there is no 'use by'
date or 'best before' date anywhere in sight, so Jesus still
expects us to take this command very seriously and apply it
to every area of our Christian life!

The problems Jesus faces as the 'Managing Director' of
the church in the twenty-first century are no different from
those of many secular organisations that have drawn up
their own Mission Statements. We have neatly copied his fine
words, printed them out on elegant scrolls and framed them
behind non-reflective glass and then hung them and hidden
them down some rarely used and dimly lit corridor of the
church. We walk past it each day as we busy ourselves about
'the Lord's work' but never hang around long enough to
allow it to influence our daily working practice. As a result,
when he comes to examine our work, he has difficulty seeing
any of his original specification in it. When he asks the
workers, 'What is the main purpose for our existence as the
church in this city?' he receives many different answers. 'We
are here to worship you. That is our main purpose for being
here.' 'We are here to meet the needs of the flock', or 'We are
here as a resource to the community, or to the wider body',
or 'We're here to provide the best conference facilities possible in the city.'

But none of these things is found in his Mission
Statement. His Mission Statement says that we are here

primarily to make disciples, and that this is the benchmark against which he will assess all the 'busy-ness' of the church. And so when he looks at everything else that we are so energetically doing 'in his name', he is faced with a choice. He either has to change his Mission Statement to fit what is being produced by his 'organisation', or he has to change the organisation so that it begins to produce the things he expects it to produce in line with his original Mission Statement. Closing down the church and simply starting all over again from the beginning is not an option. His word never changes, nor will it fail to accomplish the purpose for which it was first sent (Isaiah 55:11) and so the Mission Statement has not changed for over 2,000 years, nor will it ever do so this side of eternity.

Jesus' Mission Statement is known as the Great Commission – in other words it is a 'co-mission'; a mission that can only be accomplished in co-operation with us! He needs us in order to get the job done and we need him in order to make the job possible. Since his word never changes, and he still intends that we should be the ones who accomplish what he is longing for, *we* must be changed so that in turn we can change what we are doing and start producing what he has always wanted – disciples!

Core values

As Lois and I looked at our church in the light of Jesus' Mission Statement we realised that there were many things that needed to change before we came anywhere near to producing the kind of disciples Jesus was looking for. Some of the things that we were most familiar with needed to be reassessed by holding them up against the Great Commission, and if they weren't producing the kind of disciples Jesus wanted we knew that only a radical approach would get us back on course. But equally we knew that unless there was something to replace these familiar things with, all we would be left with would be a pile of rubble. As we examined the church, looking for areas of fruitfulness and potential fruitfulness, we knew that certain important elements needed to be in place in order that the construction could continue as God intended. These elements were numerous and were to act as the cement and nails of the vision God had entrusted to us to build, but among the more important ones were the following three 'core values'.

1. *Everyone can be a leader*

Before we look at this core value it is important that we don't read what it doesn't say! 'Everyone *can* be a leader' is not the same as saying 'Everyone *is* a leader', at least not in the sense in which we are using the word 'leadership'. We must therefore first define what we mean by 'leadership' before this core value makes very much sense at all, and it is best summed up by a statement that has become something of a catchphrase in our church: 'Leadership is not a position occupied but an influence exercised'.

All too often we associate leadership with having 'a name on a door'. 'This is Pastor Buck's office,' we say reverently as we walk past the hallowed portal. 'He has twelve degrees in theology, a diploma in advanced counselling and is one of the few people who *really* knows who the 39 authors of Deuteronomy were.' All well and good, but how many souls has Pastor Buck personally seen saved and added to his church this year? How many people has his lifestyle influenced in such a way that they imitate him and in so doing become more like Jesus? When the Managing Director of the church visits Pastor Buck's study, how does his life stand up against the requirements of the Great Commission? Having a 'name on a door' is not necessarily the same as being a disciple of Jesus, nor even a leader of the church! If we set our sights on ministerial position and on having a 'name on a door' that will celebrate the fact that we are on the way to the top, we should remember the 'ministerial position' that Jesus instructed his disciples to adopt.

> Sitting down, Jesus called the Twelve and said, '*If anyone wants to be first, he must be the very last, and the servant of all.*' (Mark 9:35, my italics)

> Jesus called them together and said, 'You know that the rulers of the Gentiles lord it over them, and their high officials exercise authority over them. Not so with you. Instead, whoever wants to become great among you must be your servant, and *whoever wants to be first must be your slave* – just as the Son of Man did not come to be served, but to serve, and to give his life as a ransom for many.' (Matthew 20:25–28, my italics)

Leadership, as distinct from government, is something that we all demonstrate in our lives each day. By example, we influence others through the things we say and do, the places that we choose to go to or not to go to, and our response to circumstances as they present themselves to us. The truth is, no one is insignificant because all of us have the power to influence for good or for ill the people whom God places in our path every day of our lives. When we exert a godly influence on others we demonstrate an alternative response to that of the world that does not go unnoticed by those around us. Our example influences others far more than we often realise and when it is a response or an action that comes from a heart that is full of the love of God it becomes attractive to the saved and the unsaved alike. This is the kind of leadership we are looking for – leadership demonstrated by godly influence in the lives of others.

An influential example is the main mechanism of discipleship. Jesus commanded the apostles to make disciples by influencing others through the values that they had learned from him (Matthew 28:20). In the same way our ability to make disciples is only limited by the example that we set others, and that in turn is only limited by the degree to which we obediently follow the commands of Jesus. Jesus' ability to make disciples was unlimited because he obeyed his Father completely. Jesus heard the voice of his Father, and in obeying his word modelled a lifestyle that was radically different from anything anyone had ever encountered before. His example was not an easy one to imitate, but his godly influence produced disciples able to go and do the same; disciples who were willing to lay down their own lives and die in order to see his influence continue in the lives of others. Recognising and reminding the members of the church that they have the power to influence for good and for God is an important core value that releases the church into active service in the world. Jesus did not command a group of random strangers or a management consultancy team to go and make disciples for him. He called his own disciples – men who had learned from the example he had set them each day as he lived among them – to go out and do the same. His influence on them became their means of influence on others, and from this the early church was birthed.

At Metro Church, as we set ourselves the task of discipling those God had called us to be immediately responsible for, and then releasing them to be leaders in their own right, we saw our church rising to the challenge to fulfil the

Great Commission. The number of people getting saved increased and the church began to grow both in numbers and in maturity through those who understood the reality of godly leadership in their community.

2. Training and equipping are not optional extras

In May 1878 the leaders of the Christian Mission met together in London to read the proofs of the mission's annual report. On the front of the document were written the following words:

THE CHRISTIAN MISSION
under the superintendence
of the Rev. William Booth
is

A VOLUNTEER ARMY
recruited from amongst the multitudes who
are without God and without hope in the world

Bramwell Booth, William Booth's 21-year-old son, was immediately provoked by what he read. 'Volunteer!' he objected loudly. 'I'm not a volunteer; I'm a regular or nothing!' William Booth was deeply challenged when he heard these words and leaning forward scratched out the word 'volunteer' and replaced it with the word 'salvation'. And so the Salvation Army officially received its name. Almost 150 years later the twenty-first-century church needs to rediscover the fiery passion of these early Salvationists as well as embracing some of the principles and values that enabled their movement to see 250,000 souls saved in Britain in a four-year period.[1]

---

[1] Richard Collier, *The General Next to God* (Collins 1965), p. 120.

Perhaps most significantly we need to understand that the Great Commission will never be fulfilled if we maintain a 'volunteer' approach towards our involvement in the church. Volunteers are at liberty to change their minds when the going gets tough. Volunteers see their involvement as more of a hobby than a lifestyle. Volunteers spend more time debating concepts than obeying orders. Salvation should no more be the work of this kind of volunteer than brain surgery be left to a person who only operates at the weekend but spends most of his time fixing car engines for a living. Salvation of lost souls should not be seen as a voluntary or optional activity but as an urgent and compelling duty. Who would stand by the side of a lake and debate whether it was the right time of day or the best day of the week to save a drowning man if it was within their power to save him? Saving that man would become the immediate priority and we would expect the same for ourselves if the roles were reversed and we were the ones who were drowning. The only valid excuse that we could offer that would prevent us from diving in and saving that person would be our own inability to swim, and if we were forced to watch that person drown we would undoubtedly be strongly motivated to learn to swim from that day on!

Training and equipping the church to serve cannot be an optional extra. We need to be trained to be effective in soul-winning, to make certain that that person is added to the church, to disciple that individual according to the pattern Jesus laid down and to release them in turn to go and do the same. For many years we majored on winning souls but found that many went back into the world because of our inability to consolidate the work of salvation that had taken place. We naïvely expected the new convert to automatically become a disciple and to know how to win others for the

Lord, how to pray and live a holy life. But Jesus made no such similar assumption.

> As Jesus was walking beside the Sea of Galilee, he saw two brothers, Simon called Peter and his brother Andrew. They were casting a net into the lake, for they were fishermen. 'Come, follow me,' Jesus said, 'and I will make you fishers of men.' At once they left their nets and followed him. (Matthew 4:18–20)

It is important to note exactly what it was that Jesus said to Peter and Andrew. He did not say, 'I have *already* made you fishers of men.' He said, 'I *will* make you fishers of men.' When they decided to leave their nets and follow him they understood that they were leaving in order to be trained in the work of evangelism as one part of their lifestyle of discipleship. As we read through the Gospels we see how they were exposed to the model of evangelism that Jesus put into practice in his own life and through his influence and example were encouraged to go and do exactly the same thing themselves.

As we looked at the need for training within the church we realised that whatever we set in place would have to be entirely practical in its focus. Simply filling our heads with information that did not deepen our own personal discipleship and thereby result in new disciples being drawn in from the world was a complete waste of time. And so we began a 40-week training course that was designed to work in conjunction with the activity of the cells that we had set in place.

By and large people responded well to this and the training was broken down into three main sections. First, we covered very basic doctrine focusing on the essentials of salvation, what it means to be saved and how practically to lead someone to Christ. Then we dealt with issues of the heart that would jeopardise our own fruitfulness in evangelism and subsequent discipleship. Finally we gave practical help and advice on all aspects of leading a cell, along with strong emphasis on prayer and spiritual warfare necessary to prepare the ground of the heart of those we were asking God to save.

The specific purpose of this training was to provide basic teaching that could be used to take a recent convert and turn them into an effective cell leader by the end of the course. But one of the more interesting and unexpected responses that we encountered came when we announced that we would be holding an exam at the end of the course in order to assess how well we had communicated these values and to see how much information had been retained. Suddenly it was understood that we were being serious about this training! Some people felt threatened because they had not been 'good at exams' in the past, but we quickly realised that others felt uneasy because the 'volunteer' spirit was being challenged and a new degree of serious commitment to the task of life-saving was being sought.

Nowhere is godly leadership and training more important than when it comes to the salvation of the lost. Christian leadership is the exercise of godly influence in the life of someone else, and when it comes to leading someone to Christ it is vital that we are substantially equipped as leaders. As we talk to the person who is inquiring about salvation we are given the responsibility of influencing their eternal destiny and welfare and that is a serious matter. The seriousness of leadership, albeit in a more governmental capacity, is well described by the writer to the Hebrews: 'Obey your leaders and submit to their authority. They keep watch over you *as men who must give an account*' (Hebrews 13:17, my italics).

But Jesus was even more direct when he confronted the Pharisees about the words that they used to influence those who sought godly counsel from them but were given something quite different!

> 'You brood of vipers, how can you who are evil say anything good? For out of the overflow of the heart the mouth speaks. The good man brings good things out of the good stored up in him, and the evil man brings evil things out of the evil stored up in him. But *I tell you that men will have to give account on the day of judgment for every careless word they have spoken.* For by your words you will be acquitted, and by your words you will be condemned.' (Matthew 12:34–37, my italics)

The Greek word that is translated here as 'careless' is *argos* which means literally 'without work'. An inactive or barren word is one that does not influence usefully in a way that produces fruit. The Pharisees were incapable of speaking anything other than barren words because of the content of their hearts and so whatever advice they gave to someone searching after God their words would inevitably be worthless and 'work-less'. But as lovers of Christ we should always be ready and able to speak words that are fruitful and produce good fruit in the life of the hearer. The book of Proverbs tells us: 'The fruit of the righteous is a tree of life, and he who wins souls is wise' (Proverbs 11:30).

Fruitful words will produce life in others, enabling us to be effective soul-winners. But how will those words find their way into our spirit? Only by training and equipping in righteousness and the storing up of God's word in our hearts. His words are both spirit and life (John 6:63) and are never barren or unproductive. But without training and equipping in the correct use of those words we run the very real risk of feeling profoundly uncomfortable on the Day of Judgement when we have to give an account for every word, unproductive or otherwise, that we have spoken!

3. Men and women must work together as co-labourers

Harvest was seen as a significant event in the calendar of the Middle East in the time of Jesus. The three major Jewish festivals, Passover, Pentecost and Tabernacles, were associated with times of harvest and many laws were instituted regarding the way God wanted his people to behave at these times. The harvest was a major social event that had both spiritual and natural consequences attached to it. When God's people rebelled against him the harvest would fail, but when they obeyed his laws they were blessed with abundant harvest and at such times there was great festivity and joy. Because of the laws of inheritance each person also had a part share in the land and therefore a responsibility to tend and work it to produce a good harvest.

But perhaps the most important thing that we need to understand in our non-agricultural society was the requirement to involve the entire family at harvest time. Men and women worked alongside each other sharing in both the backbreaking labour as well as the joyful celebrations that took place afterwards. Far from being relegated to menial duties or simply 'looking after the children' while the men did all the work, the women shared equally in the harvest in order to make certain it was all gathered in and that none of it was lost. As we looked at the elements involved in harvest in the Bible we began to appreciate that some of the things we were doing in the church were not helping to reap our own harvest in the region and therefore fulfil the Great Commission.

Much has been written about the role of women in the church and not all of it has been very helpful or gracious in its content. Perhaps some of this has been because we have failed to assess our work as a church in relation to the Great Commission. Fulfilling the Great Commission requires an understanding of the process of harvest. It was not a gender or even age-specific event; it was a family event where everyone got involved. If the church is going to harvest effectively we must not make more than half the work force involuntarily redundant. In addition, we have to see that the process of salvation is only the first stage of fulfilling the Great Commission, because Jesus lays the emphasis on continuing discipleship rather than simply harvesting the grain and leaving it to rot on the ground.

Where in the Great Commission does it mention gender when it comes to discipleship? And where, for that matter, does it mention gender in regard to baptism? Did Jesus say, for example, that only male 'leaders' of churches should be responsible for baptising their disciples? No, he didn't. The only stipulation Jesus made was that those who are *making* the disciples should baptise their own disciples. If a woman leads someone to Christ by her godly influence why should that prevent her from continuing with the work of discipleship, whatever the gender of the disciple? There may be many very good practical reasons why this relationship should not continue and the discipleship element would be better continued by someone else, but we must be careful not to add to what Jesus said. Unless we think Jesus was talking exclusively to his male disciples who would only be allowed to make other male disciples then we must be willing to permit cross-gender discipleship, at least in principle. If the early disciples had not done this, then what hope would there have been for the women?

Ministering as a couple

But we realised that the implications for co-ministry in order to fulfil the Great Commission were even more far-reaching than this. God delights in using visual aids, and perhaps not surprisingly the devil has all his energies directed toward defacing and distorting them. We are told that the Father has adopted us into his family (Romans 8:15) and adoption is a powerful visual aid that allows us to see the extent of our inheritance as sons of our heavenly Father. The devil, on the other hand, hates that imagery and so in an attempt to discredit it he promotes abortion. Abort 'unwanted' babies and you have no babies to adopt, and therefore no visual aid. The same is true in marriage. Paul tells us:

> 'For this reason a man will leave his father and mother and be united to his wife, and the two will become one flesh.' This is a profound mystery – but *I am talking about Christ and the church.* However, each one of you also must love his wife as he loves himself, and the wife must respect her husband. (Ephesians 5:31–33, my italics)

The marriage relationship was designed by God to be a visual aid demonstrating the love, faithfulness and power of the church that is in love with its Lord and Saviour. As we minister alongside one another as a married couple we demonstrate the harmony, or otherwise, of our life in Christ as 'one flesh'. Not surprisingly the devil is eager to disrupt that relationship and thereby send a completely different message to the church and to the watching world.

We realised that the church had played into the hands of the devil for too long, and by obliging men and women to be separate in ministry we deprived both the body of Christ and the lost of the power that can be released when we operate as a couple. Lois and I have always enjoyed working together in ministry, but we began to see that there were things that still needed adjusting in our own lives before this was realised in the way God required. When God saw Adam working alone in the garden he said: 'It is not good for the man to be alone. I will make a helper suitable for him' (Genesis 2:18).

Eve was given to Adam to be his helper, but many men in ministry have a rather different understanding of what this means from what God originally intended! Eve was not given to Adam to help him become a 'better Adam' at her expense. Eve was given to Adam and Adam to Eve to help them become a better couple in unity together. The Book of Ecclesiastes says: 'Two are better than one, because they have a good return for their work . . . Though one may be overpowered, two can defend themselves. A cord of three strands is not quickly broken' (Ecclesiastes 4:9, 12).

It is the intertwining of the strands that produces the strength of the cord. And in the same way the Holy Spirit wants to be intricately interlaced in our marriages to bring the strength that is required to bring in the harvest.

United we stand . . .

Jesus responded to the teachers of the law who were saying that his work and teaching were of the devil: 'If a house is divided against itself, that house cannot stand' (Mark 3:25).

If we are divided as a family, in our marriage or in our ministry we cannot function effectively or efficiently in the harvest field. For this reason we explained to the church the importance of couples ministering together and the need to see our families as our most important 'first cell'. If it didn't work with our husbands, wives and children it wasn't going to work in the world either! As we taught these things we began to see a new love and respect being shown to the married women by their husbands, who in turn received the honour of their wives as they were released into ministry.

The three core values outlined in this chapter continue to have a profound effect in the church. As we have seen them adopted and modelled by successive groups of leaders within the church so God has been able to release the harvest to us in increasingly larger quantities.

LIFE APPLICATION

How many of your regular church activities line up with and work toward the fulfilment of Jesus' Mission Statement? Do any of them need to be changed? How will you set about making those changes?

'Leadership is not a position occupied; it is an influence exercised.' Whom do you influence the most? What sort of influence do you exert?

Look at each of the three core values once again. What is your reaction to each one? What might influence your reaction to them?

PRAYER

Dear Jesus, give me the courage to honestly examine my life, holding it up against the values and goals of your Mission Statement. Holy Spirit, please identify those areas in my life that need to change. Renew my mind; transform my thoughts; empower my actions. Amen.

11

Unity

May the God who gives endurance and encouragement give you
a spirit of unity among yourselves as you follow Christ Jesus...

Romans 15:5

I remember vividly the day that God called me into the ministry. It happened one evening back in the 1980s when Lois and I were attending a popular Bible week that was held every summer at the Harrogate Showground in the north of England. I went to the meeting that evening by myself while Lois stayed behind in the caravan to look after the children. From the very beginning of the meeting I knew something unusual was taking place: for a start, I just could not stop crying. I cried through the worship; I cried through the notices; I cried during the offering. I didn't know why I was crying but that didn't seem to make very much difference; I just kept on crying. That evening Terry Virgo was preaching from the book of Nehemiah using the text: '"The wall of Jerusalem is broken down, and its gates have been burned with fire." When I heard these things, I sat down and wept' (Nehemiah 1:3–4).

I knew exactly how Nehemiah must have felt! At the end of the talk, throughout which I wept continuously, Terry Virgo said, 'This is a two-part talk that I intend to finish tomorrow night. But the Holy Spirit has told me that I need to make the appeal tonight, and it's this: If you know that the walls of your city are broken down and that its gates have been burned with fire, and you know that God is calling you to rebuild the walls and refashion the gates of your city, then I want you to stand. I'm going to pray for you right now that God will enable you to do just that.' I was among the first to respond to that call, and when I returned to our caravan at the end of the meeting Lois immediately recognised that something significant had happened to me. From the moment I had heard that the walls of the city were down and the gates were burned I knew that the Holy Spirit was saying that that was true of our city back home. I also understood that God was asking me to help in the urgent process of rebuilding that had to take place. From that evening I knew I had to resign from my job in the police force and start to work for the Lord in the ministry.

God doesn't need our help, he wants our love!

One of the challenges we face whenever we hear God speaking to us is to make certain we understand exactly what he *is* saying to us and not what we *think* we hear him saying to us. There can be a very big difference between the two! Most of us have an understandable tendency to act impulsively when we hear God speak, often out of nothing more than eager enthusiasm or because we are impatient to see the word become a reality in our lives. But by doing this we can end up creating problems for ourselves and for others.

We would all do well to remember that when God speaks to us there are three stages that we should work through in order to ensure the correct implementation of the word. These three stages are revelation, interpretation and application.

The account of Abram and Sarai in the book of Genesis demonstrates what can happen when we receive the revelation from God but don't take care to interpret and apply it correctly. Abram received the revelation from God that he was to be the father of a great nation when he was 75 years old.

> The LORD had said to Abram, 'Leave your country, your people and your father's household and go to the land I will show you. I will make you into a great nation and I will bless you; I will make your name great, and you will be a blessing. I will bless those who bless you, and whoever curses you I will curse; and all peoples on earth will be blessed through you.' So Abram left, as the LORD had told him; and Lot went with him. Abram was seventy-five years old when he set out from Haran. (Genesis 12:1–4)

When he heard God speak to him in this way he must have been completely amazed. He had been waiting such a long time to become a father and all natural hope was fading, as with each passing year he and his wife became older and less able to bear children. The revelation that Abram received seemed clear enough to him but the problem came, as it so often does, when he tried to interpret that revelation in order to apply it to his life. The chief problem from Abram's perspective was that the Lord had not set any time scale on its fulfilment, but it was obvious to Abram that it couldn't be too long before it happened because neither he nor his wife Sarai was getting any younger.

In Abram's mind the fulfilment of this promise was imminent, and so as each month passed he expected Sarai to come up to him and say, 'Abram, it's happened – I'm pregnant!' His interpretation of the word was heavily influenced by an understandable impatience to see this child who had been promised to him, but in the end this impatience was to be the cause of much dispute and great disunity within his family. When Sarai failed to become pregnant in the time that his *interpretation* of the word permitted, they decided it was time to 'help God out', conceiving a plan that resulted in the birth of Ishmael – a plan that produced a great deal of unhappiness for his entire household.

> Now Sarai, Abram's wife, had borne him no children. But she had an Egyptian maidservant named Hagar; so she said to Abram, 'The LORD has kept me from having children. Go, sleep with my maidservant; perhaps I can build a family through her.' Abram agreed to what Sarai said. So after Abram had been living in Canaan ten years, Sarai his wife took her Egyptian maidservant Hagar and gave her to her husband to be his wife. He slept with Hagar, and she conceived. (Genesis 16:1–4)

Because of their faulty interpretation of the revelation of God, their application of that word was even more disastrously off the mark. The problems that sprang up in their family, with all the bitterness and disunity that ensued, were the product of Abram's plan to 'help God out'. Of course, God didn't need Abram's help – he just longed for his love and the obedience that would flow out from it. But instead of waiting for God's plan to be worked out in God's way and in God's time they acted impulsively and Hagar gave birth to a son, Ishmael. Through the misinterpretation of God's word and the misapplication that then followed, Abram was obliged to wait until he was 100 years old and his wife Sarai was 90 before the child God had originally promised to them was born.

Many times God's perfect plan for our lives can be delayed by the 'Ishmaels' that we give birth to in order to 'help God out', but not only this; significant disunity can then arise as a direct result of our impatience and disobedience to God's word to us. Not only must the revelation be from God, but the interpretation and the application of that word can only be fully understood through the ongoing process of continued intimacy with him. Far from being a needlessly complex process, or nothing more than a series of hoops that we have to jump through in order to convince God of our worthiness to receive from him, it is a reflection of God's desire for an ongoing relationship with us – something that requires daily investment and maintenance on both of our parts. It is at this stage that we often fall short and thereby fail to understand his will for our lives.

Taking the city

I was so challenged by God's call to rebuild the walls of my city, and so enthusiastic to see its gates repaired, that I made the mistake of believing that God had entrusted this work exclusively to me. The revelation that I had received at the Bible week had been very clear but my interpretation and application of it began to produce problems as soon as we planted the church in Sunderland.

With hindsight, I realise that God had not called me to take the city in isolation and that his plan, which is the same for every city in every age, was to involve the other churches in conjunction with ours to achieve his goal. But at that time, while I may have given assent to this idea with my lips, I think I preferred to believe that I was God's particular choice for the city of Sunderland. The other churches were welcome to join in and help us in the task, but they would be helping *us* because God had called *our church* to 'rebuild the walls' of *our* city.

As you can imagine, this attitude did little to foster the

spirit of unity among the church and the churches in Sunderland! It was many years before God had worked on my heart sufficiently for me to understand that he only ever sees the church collectively in a city and not the churches as separate items. Our church was only one of the many congregations of the church of Jesus Christ in the city of Sunderland represented by various denominations, each with their own distinctive beauty in the eyes of God.

Paul wrote these words to the church in the city of Ephesus:

> His intent was that now, *through the church, the manifold wisdom of God should be made known* to the rulers and authorities in the heavenly realms, according to his eternal purpose which he accomplished in Christ Jesus our Lord. (Ephesians 3:10–1, my italics)

The Greek word that is translated as 'manifold' is *polupoikilos*, which has no direct English equivalent. The Amplified Bible gives the following expanded definition of this word: 'The complicated, many-sided wisdom of God in all its infinite variety and innumerable aspects', but perhaps for simplicity's sake we should call it the 'multi-faceted wisdom of God'. And it is this multi-faceted wisdom that is to be demonstrated through the church.

Two important concepts arise from this verse that we needed to apply to our situation in the city. First, the multi-faceted wisdom of God is demonstrated by the church (singular) and not the churches (plural) in the city. Unity among the denominational congregations of the church in a city is essential if God's wisdom is to be clearly understood by the rulers and authorities in the heavenly realms over that city. Since Jesus has become the wisdom of God for us (1 Corinthians 1:30) there is a direct link between unity in the church and the revelation of the saving power of the gospel through Jesus Christ to the people in the city. When the churches function together as the church in the city the gospel can be communicated with power and our evangelistic efforts will bear much more fruit.

Second, the wisdom of God is multi-faceted. Rather like a diamond that is made more beautiful by the facets that have been cut into it so that its true beauty can only be seen by examining it from its many sides, so too the beauty of the church is dependent upon the 'cut' of the denominational facets. Each facet plays an important role in the appreciation of the full beauty of the diamond and each facet must be accurately aligned with its adjacent facet for this to occur. Since each facet represents one aspect of the whole truth as revealed in Jesus, there is never an occasion when we can say to another group of believers in our town or city, 'We don't need you,' without compromising the effectiveness of the gospel to reach the lost.

It is only as we begin to work together in unity as the church of Jesus Christ that the city will have begun to have its walls rebuilt and its gates repaired. God had yet to intervene powerfully in the heart of his church in Sunderland, and perhaps in my heart in particular, to make this rebuilding process even a possibility.

Unity in the church

The sad fact is that there is too little unity of the kind that the Father is looking for to enable him to change the cities in which we live. He looks for his church in the city, but finds fragmented and divided groups pursuing their own vision to the exclusion of all else. While divisions caused by differences of opinion exist within the church that are serious enough to bring separation and isolation to its members, the power of the cross of Christ is limited in its ability to change our society.

Paul described the party spirit that had invaded the Corinthian church and that was linked to the personality cults that had emerged around Peter, Apollos and himself.

> My brothers, some from Chloe's household have informed me that there are quarrels among you. What I mean is this: One of you says, 'I follow Paul'; another, 'I follow Apollos'; another, 'I follow Cephas'; still another, 'I follow Christ.' Is Christ divided? Was Paul crucified for you? Were you baptised into the name of Paul? . . . For Christ did not send me to baptise, but to preach the gospel – not with words of human wisdom, lest the cross of Christ be emptied of its power. (1 Corinthians 1:11–13, 17)

Paul was eager to have them understand that while anyone other than Christ was made the centre of their attentions and the source of their corporate identity, they effectively emptied the cross of its power and therefore the hope of salvation for the people in the city of Corinth. Since the source of their party spirit seemed to revolve around exactly who had baptised whom, Paul stressed the fact that he had not been sent primarily to baptise people, thereby causing division, but to preach the gospel which has the power to unite the church. Unity in Christ is an essential prerequisite for the effective evangelism of our cities and only when the cross of Christ alone is central to both our separate and corporate church activities can we ever hope to see the numbers that we dream about saved.

Unity must be purposeful

Satan hates unity in the church. He always works to oppose the plan and purpose of God and God always has purpose in everything he plans to do. So our adversary would hardly spend the time he does creating so much disunity if unity were just a nice concept without any practical relevance in the salvation war. Unity in itself is no threat to the devil, but the purpose of God that unity promotes and the devastating power that it releases against the devil's dominion and his sphere of influence is terrifying to him. The psalmist wrote about it in Psalm 133:

> How good and pleasant it is when brothers live together in unity! It is like precious oil poured on the head, running down on the beard, running down on Aaron's beard, down upon the collar of his robes. It is as if the dew of Hermon were falling on Mount Zion. For there the LORD bestows his blessing, even life for evermore.

When we dwell together in unity the blessing that is commanded is not primarily for our benefit, but for the benefit of the lost. It is not so that we feel nice and comfortable or can all manage to sing from the same song sheet together at last; it is so that salvation can be released in our city in proportion to our unity. When the church in a city is united, salvation can be commanded by God and the people of the city can be delivered from the power and death grip of the devil. Unity is a vital ingredient in the salvation of a city – it's no wonder that Satan does his best to prevent it.

An easy target

For the church in the city to be working together in unity it is clear that certain things must change. But whenever change or the threat of change confronts the church there will almost inevitably be some who find the need to oppose the 'new' thing, boldly declaring it to be 'not of God' and confidently asserting that in strenuously opposing it they are merely 'contending for the faith'. More often than not this only has the effect of polarising views even further, with those in favour of the 'new' thing adopting one extreme position and those opposing it taking an equally extreme, but opposite, position. For a while both camps lob Bible verse encrusted hand-grenades at one another, in the hope that one might actually go off in the opposition's face and do them some real harm, and with time attitudes harden until any likelihood of communication between them becomes something almost impossible for either side to contemplate.

The media take particular delight in giving great exposure to any disagreements of this kind that stem from minor or peripheral doctrinal variance between leaders in the church, and rising to the bait well-intentioned but badly motivated apologists enter the ring to publicly slug it out with their brother or sister while the world cheers them on. Rather like modern-day gladiators, although this time with willing volunteers, they get ready to fight to the death if necessary, as long as their interpretation of doctrine or practice can triumph over that of their adversary.

Somewhere in the middle of all of this, both sides have forgotten that Jesus said: 'By this all men will know that you are my disciples, if you love one another' (John 13:35). If our love for one another is the means by which the world can identify the disciples of Jesus, then unity must be the fruit of that love, for we cannot be at one with someone we hate.

Jesus prayed for unity – so it must be important!

On the night before his crucifixion Jesus went to the Garden of Gethsemane. There he spent time praying for his disciples: those who were supposed to be praying with him but who had fallen asleep, and those who were later to become his disciples through their godly influence. He prayed:

> 'My prayer is not for them alone. I pray also for those who will believe in me through their message, that all of them may be one, Father, just as you are in me and I am in you. May they also be in us so that the world may believe that you have sent me. I have given them the glory that you gave me, that they may be one as we are one . . .' (John 17:20–22)

Few people would disagree that unity is something the church needs to both experience and demonstrate, but even fewer understand what that unity really is. What things, for example, need to be in place before the church can be truly united together? Anyone who has ever attempted to work alongside churches of differing traditions will understand some of the complexities that the quest for 'unity' introduces. The word 'unity' simply means different things to different people, and that inevitably produces different expectations and goals among those who want to work together 'in unity'.

Down through the years different groups within the church have attempted to address this in a variety of ways; some more successfully than others. But most of the problems we face with the other church or churches that we want to work alongside have more to do with the way in which we apply our doctrine in our own church or denominational setting than the basic belief enshrined in that doctrine. Styles of worship are usually the most obvious and emotive cause of difficulty. Charismatic and Pentecostal churches feel hidebound and stifled when asked to sing from a hymnbook and follow a written liturgy, whereas reformed evangelical churches feel uncomfortable with the lack of dignity and 'unwritten' liturgy that many Pentecostal churches insist upon. But both would agree that worship is something God seeks (John 4:23). And both, for that matter, would give their wholehearted backing to the statements of faith found in the Apostles' Creed.

The problems arise not so much from the belief that worship is an activity sought by God as the manner in which it is practised. The outcome of joint ecumenical meetings of this kind is usually less than satisfactory, as neither tradition feels it has encountered God because of the degree of compromise it has had to endure in what turns out to be a 'lowest common denominator' service.

So what can be done to bring us purposefully together? How can Jesus' prayer for us to 'be one . . . so that the world may believe that you have sent me' ever come to pass? Surely we will never be able to reach a compromise that will enable all denominations and traditions to feel happy at the same time? It might surprise you to hear that this is absolutely true. We will never find a style that will satisfy everyone, but that doesn't actually matter. The kind of unity Jesus longs for is not based on style or common practice, it is based on something far simpler and more fundamental than this.

What do we mean by unity in the church?

One of my friends has twin daughters, Rachel and Naomi. When they were two years old something happened to them which illustrates both the challenge of unity and the basis for its existence in the church. My friend was sitting in his armchair one day keeping one eye on his children and the other on the news report he was trying to watch on the television, while they happily played with their toys on the floor. Suddenly the peace was shattered as one of the twins decided she wanted full possession of the toy the other twin was claiming as her own. Within a moment the two girls were laying into each other as only toddlers can. He knew he had to do something to intervene but in that split second before taking any action he realised he had a choice between taking a stern, authoritative approach or a more gentle, loving and fundamentally distracting approach that would hopefully diffuse the situation. He opted for the latter and rose from his chair, scooped the flailing infants into his arms and sat back down in the armchair with one child on each knee where he began to cuddle them into himself. He firmly, but gently, kept them apart and began to tell them how much he loved them both and within a few seconds they had quite forgotten the toy over which the dispute had arisen and were enjoying the affection and attention of their father.

Then a profound thing began to happen. One of the twins reached out her arm and began to tickle the other, who responded in kind, tickling her sister with equal vigour. Before too long the girls were laughing uproariously and were now almost oblivious to their father, on whose knee they were still sitting. In the atmosphere of security and love that their father brought them, the previous squabble was a thing of the past and they were now happy to be with one another again.

The parallel with the church is obvious. Unity does not come as a result of winning arguments about ownership of 'the truth'; it comes from appreciating that we have the same Father, who loves us equally despite our differences of opinion. In fact, it is only when we are aware of our common heritage, that 'our' Father is the same as 'their' Father, that we can truly appreciate the other person or church for who they are and learn to love them as our Father loves them: unconditionally and freely.

Unity has to start somewhere

This principle of unity that can only be experienced as we appreciate our Father together was powerfully demonstrated to us during the move of God that took place in our church in 1994. Inside the church building the presence of God was almost tangible. The moment you walked in you could feel his presence and with his presence his amazing love for each one of us. As the weeks went by thousands of visitors came to the church from all over the world and from almost every denomination, and dramatic testimony after dramatic testimony was shared as hurting lives were healed and broken relationships mended. People stood up each night to share with the congregation how the Father had spoken to them and reassured them of his love for them and how they had fallen in love with Jesus all over again. Marriage relationships were restored as people came out for prayer only to discover their estranged partner standing next to them, and reconciliation took place between pastors and the people who had left their church, often with great hurt and unhappiness.

But outside the building in the cold and rain of those early winter evenings some of our brothers and sisters sat in cars praying against what they saw as the evil that was taking place inside. They had not actually been into the church to experience things for themselves but the rumours were serious enough to convince them that what was taking place in the church was demonically inspired and part of the great end-time deception. On particularly inclement nights we arranged for tea and coffee to be taken out to them as they sat in their cars and to invite them inside so that they could see what was really taking place, but inevitably they declined.

If they had summoned up the courage to join us they

would certainly have seen some unusual sights! I remember one night in particular when several nuns, dressed in their habits, came to the service and were later seen doing 'carpet time', lined up neatly next to Methodists, Baptists, Anglicans and Salvationists to name but a few. During those days no one bothered what denominational flag they normally gathered around; they just knew God was there and that was all that mattered. We also recognised the prophetic symbolism of an entire church lying on the carpet: when you're lying on your back (or front!) almost everyone is the same size! Baptists are no bigger in God's eyes than Pentecostals, Anglicans no more significant than Methodists or Brethren. The Holy Spirit was beginning the long-awaited process of uniting the church in the city of Sunderland and it was wonderful to see it happening as fears and insecurities in church leaders were melted away by the love of the Father.

Unity must have a purpose

While the devil does not want unity in the church, he is willing to tolerate unity as long as it remains purposeless. Think of it like this: if you had lived long enough in an isolated house built somewhere in the middle of a peaceful rural setting, the last thing you would want to happen would be for a builder to construct a house on the opposite side of the road that would obstruct your view of the beautiful countryside. You might, however, be willing to tolerate it, albeit grudgingly, provided that no one ever moved into it. Your worst nightmare would be for that house to be overrun with screaming children playing football in the road, and teenagers listening to loud music until late at night. As long as the house did not fulfil its purpose (occupation) you might be able to tolerate the blot on the landscape that it had become. In the same way, the devil does not like unity between church leaders, but provided it goes no further than a weekly or monthly prayer meeting then it might spoil his view but he won't feel obliged to move out and go and live somewhere else.

During those days of renewal the church leaders in Sunderland, as well as those from further afield, repented of their parochial and proud views to one another and this paved the way for the start of purposeful unity in the city. Even today, many years later, ministers from different backgrounds and practices continue to meet together regularly for prayer and to receive the strategies of God for the salvation of the city.

'Jesus said: "But I, when I am lifted up from the earth, will draw all men to myself." He said this to show the kind of death he was going to die' (John 12:32–33). It is only as the united church of Jesus Christ in a city lifts up the Saviour before the people, making his cross central to their joint cause and the salvation of the lost their combined responsibility, that Satan's power can be comprehensively broken and the eviction notice served on his dominion. Having previously made the mistake of trying to do this by ourselves, we were eager not to make the same mistake again. And so we made every effort to work alongside the other congregations in the city so that Jesus could be lifted up by us all and so that the work of salvation would not be impeded in any way.

LIFE APPLICATION

Consider the last time you received a word from God. What did you do with that revelation? Did you act on it immediately, or did you continue to seek his face for his interpretation and application?

Be honest with yourself. What is your attitude toward the 'church down the road'? What are the conditions that you would want to have met before you would be willing to work alongside them for the sake of the gospel? In the light of what you have just read in this chapter, are they the same as God's conditions for working with them?

How much do you rely on having agreed upon 'common doctrine' as described in this chapter before being willing to work with a neighbouring church that has a different denominational affiliation? How much does this influence your acceptance of them as equals in God's family?

PRAYER

Father, your Son said, 'By this all men will know that you are my disciples, if you love one another.' I want to be a true disciple of Jesus. Please give me your love for your church in my city so that we may become effective in evangelism and a source of great pleasure to you. Please help me to continue to make the 'main thing' the main thing. For Jesus' sake, Amen.

12

Mission Impossible?

*'In the last days, God says, I will pour out my Spirit on all
people. Your sons and daughters will prophesy, your young men
will see visions, your old men will dream dreams.'*

Acts 2:17

What do you dream about? I'm not referring to the haphazard assortment of bizarre images that cross your subconscious when you are fast asleep at night, but the longings and desires of your spirit that you find yourself drawn towards and thinking about whenever you have a spare moment. Our dreams are really an extension of our heart's desire reaching out into the future, the distant landmarks on the horizon that draw us onward and enable us to negotiate life with a sense of purpose. Business people dream about new products, new territories, new conquests. Artists dream of new paintings, new media, new ideas that will better express their emotions. Sports people dream of new trophies, new prize money, new levels of expertise. So what do you dream about?

Dreams and visions are important in the life of every disciple of Jesus. Whether they are literal dreams that we experience while we are asleep, or visions like the one given to Peter in Acts 10, or simply the 'dreams and visions' given by God that focus our energies into fruitful endeavour in the kingdom, they are important elements in the life of the believer who wants to fulfil his or her potential in God.

Over the last few decades the church has been encouraged to be open to God speaking to us through dreams and visions of both types. We know that 'where there is no vision the people perish' (Proverbs 29:18 KJV) and so we earnestly seek God for the vision that he has in his heart for our churches; his vision that will keep us alive and growing in a healthy way. We are encouraged to 'dream the dreams of God' which are always much bigger than ours, in the sure knowledge that he can do immeasurably more than we can ever ask or imagine (Ephesians 3:20).

And the dreams of God, as opposed to the selfish desires of man that we may sometimes convince ourselves are one and the same, represent the challenge that God places on our lives both individually and corporately to fulfil our destiny in him. They are the distant, or not so distant, landmarks on the horizon that help to keep us on the right track here and now. They are not optional; they are essential if we are to move on from where we are today to where he wants us to be tomorrow with him.

What are we going to *do* about it?

If we are honest, we have become quite good at dreaming. We dream of our church, currently populated by the same 50 people that have attended it for the last ten years, full of new converts praising God with all their heart. We dream of our cities won for Christ and the football stadiums resounding to the cheers of the crowd applauding their Saviour. We dream of thousands streaming forward for salvation and of hundreds being healed of disease and set free from demonic strongholds. We dream of the masses being touched by the genuine power of God and encountering the reality of a Father who loves and cares for them unconditionally. And these are wonderful dreams. The problem that we all face, however, is just what exactly we should be *doing* with those dreams. How does the dream become a reality? It is one thing to dream of lying on a sun-drenched beach in the Caribbean, but quite another thing to actually get there and in so doing make your dream come true.

For dreams to become reality, first of all action is required, and with the action there must be a willingness to accommodate change. And second, there must be a clear recognition that there is always a price to be paid and therefore the need for a willingness to pay it.

This is where things become difficult for the Western church. The Western church, encouraged to 'dream the dreams of God', has become bed-bound, happy to remain in the comfortable warmth of its safe environment and quite unwilling to stir itself in order to make the dreams it has been given by God become reality. The thought of getting up out of bed, putting their work clothes on and going out and doing something to make the 'dream' happen is too much for most Christians to contemplate. They would prefer instead to roll over, pull the bedclothes up a little higher and go back to sleep. 'At least this way,' they reason, 'we might have another nice dream.'

For those not afflicted in this way, and who are willing to get up and do something in order to realise their dream, there is yet another obstacle to overcome. The dream is compelling, but the present reality is depressing. When we look at where we are and the natural resources that are available to us, and then we look at the obstacles we will have to overcome in order to make the dream come true, we find ourselves almost unavoidably losing heart. How will that dream of thousands being saved ever come to pass when a quick glance at our newspapers and television screens portrays so vividly what we are up against? The strength of the current that is against us is so strong that we doubt we could ever make any headway upstream and only the most courageous, or perhaps foolhardy, would attempt to swim against it. Many who start out with good intentions end up finding the going too tough and letting the current take them wherever it wants them to go. Our dream may be to 'Go and make disciples' but with the kind of opposition we seem to face from the world it's not difficult to be persuaded that our mission appears to be impossible!

Lessons from the past

C.H. Spurgeon, the great evangelist and preacher, once said that preachers should 'preach with the Bible in one hand and the newspaper in the other'. Whether we see ourselves as preachers or not we would all do well to take note of what he had to say. We cannot afford to be ignorant of what is going on in the world but should always be able to hold those world events up against the gold standard of the word of God and say, 'This *may* be what is happening in society, but *this* is what God has to say about it.'

More than ever, the church must become like the sons of Issachar who 'understood the times and knew what Israel should do' (1 Chronicles 12:32). God is looking for us to be both willing and able to speak his life-changing word into our society. After all, it is the church that is in possession of the truth revealed in Christ Jesus – not the world; the truth that can bring God's light to the darkest of souls. We are not supposed to hide it away under a bowl but bring it out into the room so that everyone can benefit from its light

(Matthew 5:14–15). But instead we look at the state of the world and rather than boldly declaring God's heart into the situations that confront us, we just roll over and give up, failing to find our strength in God and his strategy for the redemption of our town, city or nation. Because we have focused on the depressing state of world affairs rather than on the hope that is ours in Jesus, we are obliged to construct a theology around our inability to influence society in the way we know we really should.

Over the years many of us have developed something of an 'airlift' mentality to help us cope with our ineffectual behaviour as the church. We meet together each week in our dwindling numbers in the desperate hope that we will be able to survive in the face of overwhelming evil until the day Jesus comes back to rescue us and whisk us off to be with him in heaven. 'Hold the fort, the Lord is coming' we sing encouragingly to one another as we do little more than tread water while watching helplessly as another one of our neighbours goes down for the third and last time. 'The whole world is full of wickedness,' we conclude, 'and under the power of the Evil One, so what else could we expect to happen – and what could we have done about it anyway?' When we start to think like that the mission has already become impossible. Perhaps it is time we began to read our newspapers a little less and our Bibles a whole lot more!

Going over the 'birth plan'

One day as Jesus left the Temple he began to talk to his disciples about the state of the world prior to his return.

Jesus answered: 'Watch out that no-one deceives you. For many will come in my name, claiming, "I am the Christ," and will deceive many. You will hear of wars and rumours of wars, but see to it that you are not alarmed. Such things must happen, but the end is still to come. Nation will rise against nation, and kingdom against kingdom. There will be famines and earthquakes in various places. All these are the beginning of birth-pains.' (Matthew 24:4–8)

Jesus was very open about the fact that prior to his return evil would increase, that the love of many would grow cold and that natural and political disruption would take place on an unprecedented scale throughout the whole world. But he was equally clear in pointing out that when these things took place they would be the spiritual equivalent of the pains experienced by a woman going into labour; pains that become progressively stronger and more frequent until the birth of the new life.

Whenever I read these verses I get encouraged. Many of these events are already beginning to take place in the world: the world *is* in a sorry state; the devil has a great influence in almost every walk of life, and our own nation is on a moral decline that is so steep and swift that it is more terrifying than a vertical drop roller-coaster ride. But Jesus was saying these things to his disciples in order to encourage them and not to discourage them; to give them hope not to make them despair.

Now I am led to understand that the start of labour is just the beginning of what can be an increasingly painful process and that it can be a time of great apprehension for the mother-to-be. To try and allay fears about what might happen, the experienced midwife explains the whole process from beginning to end so that the expectant mother will be less likely to fear the unknown, and better able to estimate what stage she has reached in the whole process of childbirth. It is very useful to have information like this, even if it describes some of the more negative and unpleasant aspects of the labour, because ignorance opens the door to fear. Wise explanation prepares the mother for the excitement of the new life that will soon be hers to enjoy, while acknowledging the discomfort that must be endured first. But when all the effort and pain of the labour is over and the baby is placed in the mother's arms, how many mothers would rather talk to you about the labour pains than show you their new child? None at all! The labour pains, painful as they were, are now a thing of the past and the all-consuming centre of attention is now firmly fixed on the new life that the mother holds up proudly for everyone to see.

Spiritual midwifery

Jesus was being a good spiritual midwife to his disciples, explaining every stage of the delivery and trying to allay their fears by making the unknown known.

While there was much information to be shared with them about the process of the 'birth', the focus of his talk was not so much the birth itself as the joyful end result – eternal life with him. How is it then that the church gets so fixed on the apparently negative aspects of what is going to happen rather than the joyful end result? We should be living in the daily expectation of his return, but more often than not we find ourselves worrying and entirely focused on the labour pains which sound so unappealing. Let's look further at what Jesus had to say.

And now for some really good news!

Jesus finished off his 'birth plan' with the following optimistic words:

As it was in the days of Noah, so it will be at the coming of the Son of Man. For in the days before the flood, people were eating and drinking, marrying and giving in marriage, up to the day Noah entered the ark; and they knew nothing about what would happen until the flood came and took them all away. That is how it will be at the coming of the Son of Man. Two men will be in the field; one will be taken and the other left. Two women will be grinding with a hand mill; one will be taken and the other left. Therefore keep watch, because you do not know on what day your Lord will come. (Matthew 24:37–42)

Now why are these words so optimistic? What possible encouragement could there be in hearing about people being left behind only to receive the sudden judgement that will come upon the world? Why should the church of Jesus Christ take heart as we approach these times when we read this? Isn't it an indication of our future failure rather than our success? Don't these words simply underline the impossibility of the mission Jesus has left us to complete?

To answer these questions, we should first remember that these are the events that Jesus said would literally take place at his return. He didn't say to his disciples, 'Please understand I'm only talking allegorically here!', or 'Here's another good parable for you to wonder about.' He described literal events that would take place. If we can believe that what he says is true (and we've got problems if we can't!), then we should also ask ourselves this question: 'When Jesus returns, what percentage of people, according to this passage, will be taken to be with him?' The answer may surprise you: 50 per cent of the people referred to in this passage will be taken to be with Jesus when he returns. Half of the people at work in the field and half of the people at work in the town or the city will be taken to be with him.

This percentage is used again in the corresponding passage in Luke 17. According to this passage, while many may suffer the awful judgement that suddenly befell Sodom, Jesus uses the same proportions as before for those who will be saved at his return: two people will be in bed, one will be taken and one left. In all of the examples Jesus used there is no allowance made for anything less than 50 per cent of the people being taken to be with him. Or consider it another way. Jesus could have said, 'Two thousand will be working in the field; one will be taken and 1,999 will be left,' and the way things are in the church at the moment that might be somewhat nearer the mark – but that is not what Jesus said.

Now I would like to think that 50 per cent was something of a conservative estimate, but even if it were the exact percentage of people who would go to be with Jesus, it is a long way different from our current experience in the church. In my city alone that would mean 150,000 of the 300,000 people who live here would already be saved and members of the church of Sunderland by the time Jesus returned! Just think about it! There simply wouldn't be enough space in our combined present facilities to make a traditional Sunday service even a remote possibility with a church of this size.

According to Jesus, far from it being a time for the terrified but faithful small body of the believing remnant to be airlifted to eternal safety, this will be a period of great rejoicing as the bride of Christ, the church, made up of countless millions of believers, is taken to be with her Lord. Jesus' words are so encouraging because, among other things, they point to a church that is far more effective in saving the lost than the church we see active at present.

As it was in the days of Noah

Second, Jesus said that when he returned it would be like the 'days of Noah'. Now we all know what the days of Noah were like, don't we? Well, do we? The account of the life of Noah is found in Genesis 6:

> The LORD saw how great man's wickedness on the earth had become, and that every inclination of the thoughts of his heart was only evil all the time. The LORD was grieved that he had made man on the earth, and his heart was filled with pain . . . Now the earth was corrupt in God's sight and was full of violence. God saw how corrupt the earth had become, for all the people on earth had corrupted their ways. So God said to Noah, 'I am going to put an end to all people, for the earth is filled with violence because of them. I am surely going to destroy both them and the earth. So make yourself an ark of cypress wood; make rooms in it and coat it with pitch inside and out.' (Genesis 6:5–6, 11–14)

There are some very obvious similarities between our day and Noah's day when we look at this passage, but not all of them are bad! It is obviously true that Noah's days were evil and that our days are evil as well. If there had been newspapers in Noah's day their content would have been universally wicked. Sin had become a lifestyle for the people, and with sin came death. There was murderous violence in the air as men and women took a perverse delight in creating new ways to sin against God and against one another. The same is sadly true today. The sin of the people in Noah's day caused God great pain and anguish, as our sin still causes him great anguish today.

But perhaps the Father's greatest sorrow came from the hardness of heart caused by their persistent sinfulness that produced an inability on their part to hear his cries of sorrow as they rang out around the universe. The Father's heart was broken as he saw the outworking of sin tearing his beloved creation apart limb from limb. The maggoty corruption caused by their sinfulness that ate away the flesh of their rotten hearts was a stink in his nostrils that was unbearable. At times of extremity like these, God does the only thing that he can to bring about change – he brings the old to an end and starts with the new.

The days of Noah

The Father longed for someone who still had the ability to hear the cry of his heart, who would be obedient to his will and through whom he could save the world, and he found Noah (Genesis 6:8). We should not be surprised that he still longs to find men and women who hear his great fatherly heart-cry and offer their lives in order to save the lost by showing them Jesus. Of course, it is true that unbridled evil will increase before his return – Jesus said so himself, and when we look at our society that's the way we seem to be heading. But equally we know that in its own way it will herald the change that we all long for – the return of Jesus Christ. These are the birth pains that Jesus was talking about.

It is also very important that we take careful note of the words that Jesus spoke when teaching his disciples. According to Jesus, despite their appearance these were not the 'days of unprecedented evil and wickedness', nor were they the 'days of failure for the plans and purposes of God' – these were 'the days of Noah', the preacher of righteousness (2 Peter 2:5). Despite the wickedness and hatred of God that were all around in that society, this was still the day of hope and salvation. And since the day of Jesus' return will be like the days of Noah, then, despite the evil that we may see all around us, we have no reason to be discouraged. The day in which we now live is the day of God's people, the church, who hear his heart-cry and are willing to be used like Noah in the salvation of mankind. Satan would like us to think otherwise by making us focus on his achievements in multiplying sin, but Jesus makes it clear that the church is not a redundant concept – we are his bride. This is our day and it will herald his return. That's got to be good news!

Something had better change!

Think about your town or city. What would a church of 150,000 or 200,000 or half a million people look like? You may not be able to imagine it, but you could be certain that it would look a lot different from the church you are currently committed to! Some may already have decided that a church of that size, even if it were possible, would be a freak occurrence rather than something that could ever be expected to exist near you, let alone have you as an active member. With all the current emphasis on cell church and its 'small is beautiful' approach, there is a real danger that we lose sight of the bigger picture. It is important to remember that the natural body is made up of millions of small cells that are networked together in such a way that only when they are connected to each other will there be any purposeful activity. All over the world there are cities where the church has already exceeded numbers that we might consider 'abnormal' or unique and where those who serve Jesus are no longer the silent minority of the population. Together they function in such a way that God's purposes can be fulfilled in their society. Why shouldn't that happen in our country?

When Lois and I first visited Pastor Castellanos' church in Bogota we saw firsthand how one church in a city could grow to over 200,000 members. But it was not built on organisation, programme or the charisma and drive of its leadership. Instead, it was built on the principles of humility, brokenness and death to self; principles that when implemented remove the filters through which we tend to view God's plans and which distort our perception and understanding of his will for us.

We understood early on that if we wanted to see the same growth in the church in Sunderland then we had to accept that there was no formula that could be copied or structure that could be bolted on to something we already had. Rather, it required a fundamental reappraisal of the way in which we would build the church.

This book has been an attempt to share some of these core values with you as we have begun to see the fruit of them in our own lives and in the church as it grows. One thing is certain, however: if we are going to see our cities turn to the Saviour and acknowledge him as the Lord of all, then church is going to have to take on a very different shape from the one it has at present. If we make church comfortable for Christians we cannot be surprised if we only attract Christians. And while our churches may be comfortable for Christians, complete with their own dress codes, language and music, these things are outside the experience and beyond the reach of many people in the world and make them feel entirely uncomfortable whenever they get anywhere near the front door. 'Seeker sensitivity' can become a distraction if we are not careful, but we must not forget this: the majority of the church are not yet saved! They are still living their lives as the enemies of God, ignorant of who Jesus is and what he has done for them. But if we are willing to be made uncomfortable by the Holy Spirit and build the church the way he wants it built, rather than the way we would often prefer it, we will start to see the prodigals returning, the masses being saved and growth of the kind that will prepare the way for the return of Jesus.

The church that is ready for Jesus' return

God saw something in Noah that would make possible his heart's desire to bring salvation to a sinful world. If our days and Noah's days are to have such similarity then what characteristics did Noah possess that enabled him to be of use to God that we must also demonstrate in our lives? If our day and Noah's day bear any similarity then these same characteristics must also be found in our churches.

1. Holiness

Noah found favour in the eyes of God not because he was perfect but because he was blameless: 'Noah was a righteous man, blameless among the people of his time, and he walked with God' (Genesis 6:9). He did not deliberately choose to sin but instead he chose to live differently from his neighbours. He didn't tolerate evil – he was intolerant toward it. He didn't absorb the values of his society; he stood out against them. He didn't have to be the same as everyone else; he was willing to be different.

The church that will be ready for the return of Jesus will also find favour in God's eyes, and for the same reasons. We cannot please God without personal holiness (Proverbs 11:20) and without holiness we will not be ready to meet him face to face (Hebrews 12:14). Paul tells us that we have a responsibility to get our lives sorted out before God:

'Since we have these promises, dear friends, let us purify ourselves from everything that contaminates body and spirit, perfecting holiness out of reverence for God' (2 Corinthians 7:1).

The uncomfortable truth is that when God examines our hearts he will discover that we have either 'set apart Christ as Lord', or we have simply set him aside in preference to something or someone else. The church that is ready for Jesus' return will be characterised by holiness and purity.

2. Radical obedience

'Noah did everything just as God commanded him' (Genesis 6:22). Noah was asked to build an ark that was to be 450 feet long, 75 feet broad and 45 feet high and he was given 120 years to build it! Even if he had wanted to he couldn't have hidden it very easily because it was so big and it took up so much of his time each day, quite apart from its unusual appearance, which must have made it a talking point among his neighbours. That kind of construction was an open invitation for the people in his society to get violent toward him and his family. But Noah didn't modify God's plans for salvation in order to make life more comfortable for himself; instead, he was willing to do everything God commanded him because he feared God more than he feared man. Only radical obedience to the command of Jesus to preach the gospel and to make disciples will result in salvation on the scale we dream about and God longs for.

3. Effective evangelists

'The LORD then said to Noah, "Go into the ark, you and your whole family, because I have found you righteous in this generation"' (Genesis 7:1). How do we measure successful, effective evangelism? By the number of cards handed in at the end of a crusade? By the number of new members we add to the church roll? By comparing our 'success' with the church down the street? In 2 Peter 2:5 Noah is described as a 'preacher of righteousness', but by our standards he wasn't very good at his job. In total, he saw only seven people saved in 120 years of preaching – and they were all members of his own family! But God commends Noah for his faith in Hebrews 11 because he obeyed God's word by effectively sharing his love for God and God's love for the world with those he was most able to influence. Remember that leadership is not a position occupied but an influence exercised. God's measure of effective evangelism is rather different from ours. He gives us responsibility first and foremost for those whom we are best able to influence because of our relationship with them. This is one of the reasons why we believe that cell church is the model best able to effectively evangelise our communities.

4. Friends of God

> The LORD was grieved that he had made man on the earth, and his heart was filled with pain. (Genesis 6:6)

> But Noah found favour in the eyes of the LORD. This is the account of Noah. Noah was a righteous man, blameless among the people of his time, and he walked with God. (Genesis 6:8–9)

Noah was God's friend. Friends share the deep issues of their heart with one another. The Father found in Noah the friend he was looking for, someone with whom he could share his heart that was full of pain. God is looking for a church full of men and women he can call his friends and with whom he can share his heart of love for the lost. He is looking for a church that, like Noah, is filled with his compassion and that can make a difference to a hurting and fallen world. Jesus said: 'You are my friends if you do what I command' (John 15:14). Was he talking about us?

5. *Reckless faith*

So make yourself an ark of cypress wood; make rooms in it and coat it with pitch inside and out. This is how you are to build it: The ark is to be 450 feet long, 75 feet wide and 45 feet high. (Genesis 6:14–15)

Noah was commanded by God to:

- build a structure that had never been built before
- in order to perform a function that hadn't even been dreamed of before
- for use in a climatic event that had never been experienced before
- that was to be on a global scale, the possibility of which had never been considered before.

As far as Noah was concerned, he was quite literally in uncharted waters. There were no well-established precedents and no biblical examples to follow. The project seemed incredible, but he was willing to risk humiliation because he knew what it was that his Friend had asked him to do and he wasn't going to disobey him. Noah's reckless faith made it possible for his evangelistic endeavours to bear lasting fruit! The church that is ready to welcome Jesus will be a church familiar with the unfamiliar, reckless in faith and radical in obedience.

Dismiss the crowds and build the church

When we first came back from the meeting at which Pastor Castellanos had challenged us to dismiss the crowds and build the church we knew that there were some major changes ahead of us and some uncharted waters to set sail into. What was our response going to be if God asked us to do something in Metro Church that had never been done before? What would we do if he asked us to build a structure that would save thousands of lives in the north-east, but in a style that was almost entirely unfamiliar to us? How would we respond to the criticism and opposition that a new venture like this would almost certainly provoke? Would we have the faith to build it without modifying God's plans to make life 'easier' for ourselves?

The answer to those questions still remains to be seen. But God is looking at the united church throughout our nation and he is actively searching for those whose hearts are fully committed to him (2 Chronicles 16:9) in the hope that we will have the faith and the vision to bring these things about. The principles and values that I have written about in this book are actively being implemented in our church and are beginning to bear good fruit, but we are aware that despite the magnitude of some of the changes that we have already made, there are still more to come.

Our desire is not to gather a crowd of people together and by virtue of numbers alone think we have accomplished what God requires, but rather to make disciples who in turn will be able to go and do the same, and who will be expectant and ready to welcome the Lord of glory when he returns. If this were impossible, why would Jesus have commanded us to do it?

LIFE APPLICATION

What do you dream about? Your dreams will determine your destiny.

What steps have you taken to realise those dreams? Do you expect them to fall into your lap, or are you ready for hard work and personal discomfort?

What changes have you made in order to accommodate growth? A pregnant mother prepares the baby's room before the birth and not after the baby arrives. What preparation do you still need to make?

PRAYER

Dear Jesus, thank you that you are coming back soon. Thank you that your church will be the bride you have been longing so passionately for – holy and pure, ready for the Bridegroom. I want to make myself ready for your return and I ask you now to fill me with your Holy Spirit. I want to pray with you 'that none should perish', but that all those whose lives I have the ability to influence may come to repentance. Amen.

A Word to Leaders, Present and Future . . .

'You did not choose me, but I chose you and appointed you to go and bear fruit – fruit that will last.'

John 15:16

Over the past twelve chapters I have attempted to describe some of the challenges that the Holy Spirit brought to Lois and me as we were obedient to his word to dismiss the crowds and build the church. None of these challenges has been easy to bring about, all of them involving our dying to one aspect or another of the ministry or to the security of having 'church' as we had known it all of our lives. None of these changes took place overnight and even now we are still working through many of the things that you have been reading about. We have not arrived; we have only started out on the way, with the Holy Spirit as our guide, and we certainly do not know all of the answers.

Discipleship, encountering God, the principle of honour, and unity in the church are some of the key components that we have addressed as we have begun to build the church in the 'new' way that the Holy Spirit has been leading us. Of necessity, I have not talked about many of the other important areas of church life such as evangelism, cell structure, government in the church, spiritual warfare and prayer.

Nevertheless, I have tried to set before you some of the principles we have seen successfully implemented in Pastor Castellanos' church in Bogota and which we are beginning to see produce much good fruit that will last.

I hope that you have found this book challenging, but I also hope that the Holy Spirit will be able to use some of its content to help direct the church that God has entrusted to your safekeeping in his ways.

Angels on the Walls

by Wallace and Mary Brown

What happens when a church drops its barricades against the community? Wallace and Mary Brown decided to do just that – literally. Situated in the middle of three large housing estates on the outskirts of Birmingham, with crime and vandalism all around, they stepped out in faith and took down the barbed wire and high walls. Gradually but unmistakably they saw their community begin to turn to Christ for healing and eternal life.

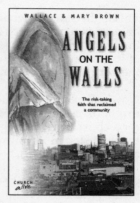

With refreshing honesty about the hard times as well as the rewarding times, this is the gripping story of how a small, defensive fellowship became a thriving church able to plant a new congregation in a neighbouring district.

CHURCH
alive

The Church in the Market Place

by George Carey

This is the story of what can happen when a church allows the Spirit of Jesus to take control of its money, its traditions and the very lives of its members.

Now complete with study guide, this book is a unique resource for a church that is looking for the next step in its journey into renewal and growth.

George Carey was for seven years Vicar of St Nicholas's, Durham, before going on to be Principal of Trinity College, Bishop of Bath & Wells and then Archbishop of Canterbury.

'It is impossible to read a book like *The Church in the Market Place* without seeing that here is a man who has placed himself entirely under God's direction.'
The Sunday Telegraph

CHURCH
alive